Elijah Baldwin Huntington

Stamford Soldiers' Memorial

Elijah Baldwin Huntington

Stamford Soldiers' Memorial

ISBN/EAN: 9783337134129

Printed in Europe, USA, Canada, Australia, Japan

Cover: Foto ©ninafisch / pixelio.de

More available books at **www.hansebooks.com**

STAMFORD

SOLDIERS' MEMORIAL,

BY

Rev. E. B. HUNTINGTON, A. M.,

AUTHOR OF HUNTINGTON FAMILY MEMOIR AND HISTORY OF STAMFORD

STAMFORD, CONN.:
PUBLISHED BY THE AUTHOR
1869.

Entered according to Act of Congress, in the year 1869, by

ELIJAH B. HUNTINGTON,

In the Clerk's Office of the District Court of the United States, for the State of Connecticut.

E. HOYT & CO., Printers,
120 William St. N. Y.

DEDICATED TO THE SONS AND CITIZENS OF STAMFORD, WHO, IN
THE HOUR OF OUR GREAT PERIL, NOBLY DEFENDED
OUR NATIONAL INTEGRITY AND HONOR.

TABLE OF CONTENTS.

PART I.—CITIZEN SERVICE .... PAGE	9
PART II.—MILITARY SERVICE	37
THIRD CONN. VOL. REGIMENT	40
SIXTH	45
TENTH	59
SEVENTEENTH	66
TWENTY-EIGHTH	73
OTHER CONN. REGIMENTS	89
NEW YORK REGIMENTS	95
REGIMENTS OF OTHER STATES	100
VOLUNTEERS ASSIGNED TO NO REGIMENT	101
UNITED STATES ARMY	102
CITIZENS WHO FURNISHED SUBSTITUTES	107
DRAFTED CITIZENS WHO FURNISHED SUBS.	108
PART III.—NAVAL SERVICE	109
PART IV.—OBITUARY	117
FAMILIES REPRESENTED BY TWO OR MORE SONS	153
INDEX TO NAMES OF VOLUNTEERS	157

PREFACE.

This STAMFORD SOLDIERS' MEMORIAL has no higher aim than to report worthily the service which the representatives of the town rendered during the recent civil war. Believing it to have been an honorable and patriotic service, it seemed to the author, due to the men who rendered it, that some record of it should be preserved. Nor did it seem less due to the credit of the town, that so important a feature of its history should be sketched while the materials for it were still within our reach. Indeed, the record which follows is but a fulfillment of the first intent of the author, in projecting the History of the town, and very appropriately follows as its supplement.

Besides, a grateful people would wish to rear some worthy memorial of services, such as we are here to record. No part of the story of Stamford has a higher claim to monumental fame. And, surely, no monument, however costly or durable, of granite or of bronze, no memorial hall, however rich or apposite, in finish or in use, could so well perpetuate such memories, as the simple story of the personal services of these our devoted and valiant citizens. In such a story, if truthfully told, the monumental hall or shaft itself, if such shall ever be reared, will find an interpreter which future generations shall better understand.

In this MEMORIAL, we have aimed to include every name which has represented the town, in the military and naval service which it is its special aim to report. No one of these names could well be spared from the list. Every one had its value in the great contribution, thus made. Even deserters had already, though unwittingly, it may have been, contributed the influence of numbers to the cause, often, when numbers have answered instead of battles.

The main sources from which the following record has been made, or verified, have been: "The Catalogue of the Connecticut Volunteer Force," which includes nearly every name representing the town in any Connecticut regiment; the Stamford *Advocate*, whose correspondence during the war was equally full and minute; the full report of Capt. Charles H. Brown, and the private diary of Noah W. Hoyt, of the 28th Conn. regiment; private letters from several of our citizens in the service; and personal conversations of scores of others of them or their friends.

Of those whose printed correspondence has been of service to the author, he gratefully acknowledges his obligation to the following contributors: J. A. Quintard, Jas. W. Daskam, Col. A. G. Brady, Gen. Wm. P. Jones, Capt. Albert Stevens, Capt. B. L. Greaves, Capt. W. B. Nichols, Capt. Chas. H. Brown, Col. Lorenzo Meeker, Dr. Wm. H. Trowbridge, Rev. P. S. Evans, Chas. A. Weed, Sergt. H. M. Capper, Lieut. Edgar Hoyt, Sergt. Chas. W. Knapp, Elbert Ayres, D. C. Comstock, jr., "C. H. C.," and "J. H. K.," 28th Conn., "J. A. H.," 4th Conn., "M. W. T.," 6th Conn., "Leinad," 10th Conn., and "W. C. G.," U. S. Steamer Rescue.

To CHARLES W. WARDWELL, Esq., another son of the town, my hearty thanks are also due, for his generous and freely offered contribution towards the expense of publishing this MEMORIAL.

For the exceedingly tasteful typographical execution of the work, our readers are indebted to Lieut. Edgar Hoyt, of the firm of E. Hoyt & Co., New York City,—himself a son and citizen soldier of the town; and for the occasional mistakes detected on these pages, there will be found abundant compensation in the general accuracy and beauty of the work.

The author in bringing these pleasant labors of months to an end would here express his heartiest thanks to the many personal friends, whose words of kindly encouragement have been a frequent benediction on his work. Never, altogether unrewarded, is any toil which draws its inspiration from the sympathy of such friends. To them, therefore, and to all the good citizens of the town, who share in the honor of every record which honors the town itself, these humble contributions to its history and patriotism are most gratefully commended by the author.

Stamford, April, 1869.

PART FIRST.

CITIZEN SERVICE.

CITIZEN SERVICE.

On the election of ABRAHAM LINCOLN, President of the United States, in November, 1860, a portion of the party which had opposed him, at once renounced allegiance to the Government, of which he was the chief executive, elect; and forthwith entered on a course of measures to establish their independence. In this emergency, Governor William A. Buckingham, of Connecticut, sought to put the State into a posture of successful resistance, and called for volunteers to fill up the ranks of our long unused militia. In response to this call, through the Adjutant-General of the State, Lorenzo Meeker, then captain of the Stamford Light Guards, issued an invitation in the *Advocate*, of January 25, 1861, to any of our citizens who wished to enlist, to meet him for that purpose, on the evening of February 1st, following. And this is the first record furnished in Stamford, having reference to the recent war. Yet it is hardly probable that a single citizen of the town, had even a faint idea that the Stamford Light Guards, or any other military company, would ever be called from the town into an actual conflict of arms.

But when on the 12th of April, 1861, organized secessionists, by an ACT OF WAR, appealed to arms, in assertion of their claims, the citizens of Stamford, at once, and unanimously, resolved to stand by the Government which they had sworn to defend.

Even those who had most vigorously opposed the election of President Lincoln, with commendable zeal now rallied, with his supporters to the defense of his authority. We agreed in the theory, that he was the nation's executive, and that his first duty as well as ours, was now to defend the nation's life.

This universal sentiment of the citizens was well expressed by one of the sons of the town, then in the city, but whose frequent letters in our local paper were to do good service for the Union cause during the conflict into which we had been plunged. On the 17th of the same month, which heard the tocsin of war sounding from rebel guns at Fort Sumpter, his stirring words were, and we had no one here who ventured or even wished to join issue with him, "American soldiers have been driven from an American fort, and the American flag has been displaced by a rebel ensign. The North has no war to wage with the South; but it has a war to wage against treason and rebellion. We have but one party among us."

Our editor, William S. Campbell, Esq., in the same issue from which we have just quoted, said what every reader felt was the exact truth : "Already party differences are forgotten. The North is consolidating its forces, and not a man with a drop of patriotic blood in his veins but rallies to the aid of his country. One thing is certain, the Government will be sustained, the call for volunteers responded to with loyal enthusiasm, and whatever be the issue of the struggle as regards the South, the North will come out of it with honor untarnished, and the Stars and Stripes will continue to wave over a free and united people."

One week later, Mr. Campbell closed a brief but earnest editorial in the same clear, ringing tones—no uncertain sound: "Let treason be rebuked, rebellion suppressed—

that is the present duty." The same issue of the *Advocate* gives us another bracing letter from the New York correspondent, already quoted, whose signature "Q" indicated the French Huguenot origin of the earnest loyalty which he expressed so well. In this letter he says: "that awful as civil war could be, the people would gladly welcome its evils, rather than submit to a disruption of the Government, and a tame capitulation to treason."

Such was plainly on the opening of this struggle, the prevailing sentiment of both political parties in Stamford. Flags were seen floating everywhere in the town—hundreds of them, testifying to this sentiment of loyalty. Conspicuous among them was the beautiful one floating over our Concert Hall; and our cannon thundered its greeting to the summons with which it stirred every patriotic heart.

The following, from our local paper, is but a characteristic record of the times; and it shows as many others which follow will show, how completely, for the time being, all party feeling had been sunk in the popular anxiety for the perpetuity of the Government of these States: "To the Brothers Scofield and Messrs. A. G. Clark & Co., belongs the credit of designing, and to the ladies is due the honor of making this flag of our country."

The tocsin of war at Sumpter, had been too distinct to be mistaken. Whatever the old political threats had meant, this left no alternative for the people; they must now either defend the Union which they had established, or consent to be broken up.

It was well for us, that at the first, both the old political parties at the North heard and heeded the call thus made upon them; and that for months but one sentiment found expression on the subject of the war. To fight was the only acknowledged duty of the hour.

On the call of the President for volunteers, April 15, 1861, Stamford was stirred, probably as never before. A meeting of the citizens was called for the following Saturday evening, to aid in raising men and means for the war. Governor William T. Minor was called to preside, and in a few earnest words, he set forth the nature of the crisis, and the need for action. John Davenport, a great grandson of that Hon. Abraham Davenport, whose name and influence were so marked in our revolutionary period, was chosen Secretary. Thomas G. Ritch, Esq., Rev. P. S. Evans, H. F. Osborn, Rev. E. B. Huntington, Jacob Kreig, G. B. Glendining, Lorenzo Meeker, and James Betts, addressed the meeting in support of the most vigorous measures.

Volunteering had already commenced. Headed by two of our young men, Thedore Miller and Theodore Delcroix, the list had already grown to about thirty names. When these names were read to the meeting, amid the acclamations of the crowded assembly, the chairman called out redoubled acclamations, by announcing the gift of a drum to them from our townsman William P. Jones, Esq., who had already tendered his services to the President.

At this meeting a committee was appointed to raise funds, consisting of Hon. James H. Hoyt, Isaac Quintard, Charles Brown, William Skiddy and Albert Seely. Four thousand and five hundred dollars were promptly pledged to the cause and it was now settled, beyond a doubt, that if called upon, the Stamford people would be found ready, with whatever ability they had, to defend the honor and integrity of our national life.

Provision was now made for raising before the people a National Flag, as a perpetual symbol of the loyalty of our citizens. The following response from one of our honored citizens is a faithful witness to the sentiment

of the whole community, and deserves its record in our
Memorial.

STAMFORD, Conn., April 23, 1861.

My Friends of the Union:—I am informed that a national flag-staff is to be erected in the centre of the village of Stamford, and having in my possession one of the trophies gained by our citizen army, under the gallant Scott, in the Mexican war, I now offer it with pleasure and pride. This truck, from the flag-staff off the castle at Vera Cruz—may it be placed on the staff to which the stars and stripes are to be hoisted under the wings of the American eagle, trusting that no other flag may ever be raised on this staff until we are exterminated.

Your fellow-countryman,

WILLIAM SKIDDY.

The writer of the above gallant offer had the pleasure on the following Fourth of July, of raising with his own hands, the National Flag to its place in the center of the village.

Meanwhile the work of raising men was going on. By Monday, April 28th, sixteen days from the first traitor shot against Sumpter, our first company, numbering thirty-nine of our citizens, summoned from their successful vocations, were pledged and ready for any service, to which the issues of the contest might lead them. They had counted the cost and were already in the lists. The roll-call had already gathered them, each at his post, for their departure for the field. Four of their number, Wells Allis, Theodore Miller, Theodore Delcroix and Peter Rooney had been appointed a committee to enroll other men as volunteers for the war, and they had rendered good service in this work.

It was an occasion of no ordinary interest which called our citizens to this first parting with their sons and neighbors. Who can tell the feelings which stirred in human affections, at that morning hour. There were not wanting womanly or manly tears, to testify to the deep feeling which ruled. The company were addressed in a brief but telling speech by Rev. P. S. Evans, of the Baptist church, and were then commended to the protection of the God of battles, in a prayer by Rev. Mr. Weed, of the Methodist church. Who those men were, our roll of honor, in Company F, 3d Connecticut Volunteers, will tell; and what service they rendered, our subsequent record of the several companies they represented will show.

During the enlistment of this first company, Captain Lorenzo Meeker, already mentioned as connected with our local militia, and who was accounted an officer of especial merit in military tactics, and a thorough master of the drill, was also busy in recruiting another company of our citizens for any call which might be made upon them. He soon succeeded in filling up the company, and early in May went to Hartford to offer their services to the Government. They were not accepted for either of the regiments then being organized, because they would not accept the conditions on which the officers were to be appointed. Many of them enlisted singly into other regiments of the State, or of New York; but with his numbers kept up, on the 5th of September, the Captain had the satisfaction of being mustered in, as Company D, of the Sixth Connecticut Volunteers, where their noble record will be found.

At the same time we were enrolling others of our citizens in Company G, of the Tenth Connecticut Volunteers, for which we furnished, before the war closed, several excellent names. And their record, also, in its appropriate place, will show some of the most effective service of the war.

To meet the necessary expenses of these war measures, a special town meeting was called for May 4th, on the request of about fifty citizens of the town, headed by William Skiddy, Joseph D. Warren and James H. Olmstead, Esq.

Of this meeting, held in the Town Hall, Wm. H. Holly, Esq., was chosen Chairman. After an earnest plea for prompt measures to supply the needed sinews of the war now begun, Mr. Holly introduced among others, the following resolution. The preamble had set forth, that the chief Executive of the State, in response to the President's call for 75,000 men, had issued his call upon the towns for volunteers; and that "many of our relations, friends and citizens have responded to the call, having gone forth to bear arms in vindication of our honor and integrity as a nation—therefore,

"*Resolved*, By the inhabitants of the town of Stamford, in special town meeting, legally warned and assembled on this 4th day of May, 1861, that a tax of one and a half mills on the dollar, of the assessment list of this town last perfected, be and is hereby levied, to be forthwith collected and paid into the Treasury of this town, to constitute a fund to defray the expenses in the foregoing preamble; also to provide pecuniary aid and relief to the families of such volunteers as have gone or may go forth in company or companies organized in this town, during the absence of such volunteers."

Stephen B. Provost, Andrew Perry, Jno. M. Hall, Josiah Smith and William Todd were a committee to audit the bills of expense already incurred, and to dispense aid to the families of our volunteers; to each man's wife three dollars per week, to each child under fifteen years one dollar, and to each widowed mother who is depending on such volunteer for her support three dollars; and the committee were authorized at their discretion, to increase these amounts to such sums as they deemed proper, in case of sickness or other urgent necessity. The resolution, after brief discussion, was unanimously passed.

Early May of this year finds also the women of Stamford earnestly at work for the comfort of our "Boys in Blue." Every church became alive with zeal to equal every other church in this pressing duty of the hour. And when it was found probable that for many months to come, perhaps for years, such organizations would be needed, the mothers and sisters of the town showed themselves ready for the consecration. One of their first offerings to the cause was a banner to lead our boys of Company F, Third Connecticut Volunteers.

Citizens who could not go to the field, organized themselves into Home Guards, and, evening after evening, submitted to such drill as might possibly help them in some future call of the country.

Even our children caught the spirit of the times. Our Graded School swung to the breeze the National Flag, one of the largest in town, to the huzzas of a multitude of children voices. Right heartily they sang the Star Spangled Banner, and without reservation pledged themselves to an undying patriotism in response to the earnest words of Rev. Mr. Evans, who addressed them.

How faithful these children were, is seen in a little incident, occurring in the early winter of 1861. A hint had been given them that our soldiers needed writing materials. The school children extemporized a box of the needed articles; and when opened for the use of the company, it was found to contain eighty-three quires of paper, seventy-five packages of envelopes, two hundred lead pencils, with rubbers, postage stamps, tracts and books. And on the fly-leaf of a neat gilt testament, some one of these children of the town, thus early comprehending at a glance the "situation," had written—"Don't return fugitives to their cruel masters."

So general was the interest in these warlike preparations,

when the national holiday of 1861 came. The National Festival of this year in Stamford is ever to be remembered for the unanimity with which our citizens re-consecrated themselves to the Union cause. The committee of arrangements for the celebration were the Hon. M. F. Merritt, Wm. P. Jones, G. K. Riker, J. A. Candee, James H. Olmstead, Edwin Bishop, James W. Daskam, Andrew Perry, and Samuel Lockwood. Mr. Merritt called the meeting to order, and Hon. Charles Hawley was appointed president. Hon. William T. Minor, Hon. Truman Smith, Stephen B. Provost, Hon. James H. Hoyt, William Skiddy, Robert Swartwout, J. W. Hubbard, Joseph B. Hoyt, William R. Fosdick, J. W. Leeds, Charles Pitt, and Theodore J. Daskam, vice-presidents. Spirited addresses were made by the Hon. Charles Hawley, Rev. William C. Hoyt, Hon. Stewart L. Woodford, Rev. R. R. Booth, and Rev. P. S. Evans. A patriotic poem also was read by Rev. Walter Mitchell; and the Star Spangled Banner was sung with fine effect by Theodore Lockwood, Sands Seely, and Isaac Wardwell, the entire audience joining in the chorus. It is hardly asserting too much, to say, that at the closing hour of these services, the vote would have been unanimous which should have pledged every man and every dollar of the town to the defense of the Nation's perpetual unity.

The following business item tells its story of the sentiment held by our business men, as to the nature and claims of the crisis which had now come. It is found in the *Advocate* of Sept. 27, 1861, and thus testifies: "Books for subscription to the National Loan were opened on Tuesday in this place by John W. Leeds, Esq., agent for the government, and in two days $34,000 were subscribed. This is in addition to subscription heretofore made by the Stamford Bank $65,000 and the Savings Bank for $45,000."

Such earnestness on the part of the people and such readiness to furnish the sinews of war, would seem to argue the speediest suppression of any rebellion which could threaten them. But we found ourselves surprised by an enemy to whom we had entrusted our readiest munitions of defense. Those whom we had specially educated for war, were largely the leaders of the secession camp. The Army of the Union was mainly under the generals of treason. The Navy had been dispersed or was stealthily seized. From our highest seats of national authority, the men who knew all our exposure had gone forth with all the influence which we had given them during their participation in the public service, to wield their knowledge and influence for traitors. Thus taken at disadvantage, we made for months and years even, but sorry headway against the formidable preparations which for years had been gathering against us.

But these months furnished the needed opportunities for our trial. We were sounding the depths of the fell purpose which had seized upon the leaders of this great treason. And, though, at times, everything seemed to go against us, we were still held together until the day for our triumph should dawn.

Already we had sent to the front more men than the most fearful of us had ever predicted we should need. Already we had supplied more money than we had supposed it within our pecuniary possibilities to spare. And yet, whenever our exposed men at the front gave out, whenever comfortable subsistence for them was wanting, we set ourselves to find the men and to supply the means.

In the summer of 1862, the government called for 300,000 more men. The following record will show in what spirit the call was met:

" The citizens of Stamford and vicinity of all parties who

are for supporting the government in its prosecution of the war against treason and rebellion, and also for devising ways and means for furnishing our quota of 300,000 men called for by the President, are requested to meet at Seely's Hall on Friday (this) evening, July 18th, 1862, at seven and half o'clock, to proffer such aid to the government as may be within our power.

"Wm. T. Minor, J. B. Ferris, A. N. Holly, Jas. H. Olmstead, Jas. L. Lockwood, B. J. Daskam, Andrew Perry, A. G. Clark, David H. Clark, Chas. Holly, Wm. S. Campbell, Chauncey Ayres, A. G. Brady and Albert Seely."

A large assembly gathered in response to this call and Oliver Hoyt was called to preside. Addresses were made by Rev. H. K. Bartlett of the Presbyterian Church, Rev. Mr. Cox a Methodist clergyman of St. Louis, and Hon. Stewart L. Woodford who had just left his residence in Stamford for one in New York. Under the effective appeals made in their addresses a large number of volunteers responded. Provision was made for holding another meeting on Thursday of the following week. According to this announcement, an immense meeting of our citizens of both sexes gathered in Seely's Hall, July 24th, 1862.

George Elder, Esq., was called to preside, with the following list of vice-presidents: Charles Hawley, Truman Smith, A. N. Holly, George A. Hoyt, S. B. Provost, William T. Minor, Oliver Hoyt, William Skiddy, Welles R. Ritch, Isaac Quintard, Joseph B. Hoyt, Theodore Davenport, John Ferguson, Smith Weed, Charles Williams, H. K. Skelding, John B. Reed, Charles Pitt, J. B. Ferris, E. P. Whitney, Thomas Crane, Charles Hendrie, William R. Fosdick, Chas. H. Starr, Morgan Morgans, James H. Hoyt, James B. Scofield, Oliver Scofield, Thomas Gardner, Seymour Hoyt, N. E. Adams, J. H. Carrington, J. W. Hubbard, J. D. Weeks,

Alfred Hoyt, S. B. Thompson, T. S. Hall, J. B. Knapp, G. F. Nesbitt, Lyman Lockwood, John Hecker, and Charles H. Scofield.

D. H. Clark, F. R. Leeds, George E. Scofield and F. M. Hawley, Secretaries.

Earnest addresses were made, all of them having the same unmistakable ring of loyalty to the Union and death to treason, by Hon. William T. Minor, Rev. Walter Mitchell, Col. William H. Noble, of Bridgeport, Thomas G. Ritch, Esq., and James H. Olmstead, Esq. In response to the call thus made upon the citizens by representatives of both political parties, $2,500 were promptly pledged, in sums ranging from $500, pledged by the Stamford Manufacturing Company, down to $5. This sum was increased to $3,000 during the following week.

The following letter from the *Advocate* of August 13, 1862, shows how successful we had been in raising men as well as means. Allen G. Brady, Esq., referred to in the letter, formerly from Torrington, but at this date in business here, had been lieutenant-colonel in the Third Connecticut Volunteers, and had been authorized by Governor Buckingham to raise a company of volunteers in Stamford.

"EDITOR OF THE ADVOCATE:—I send herewith a list of the volunteer company which will leave to-day for camp at Bridgeport. It is a list of which we may well be proud. The first name was entered on the 18th of last month, and the last on the 11th inst., making 109 names enrolled in twenty-four days.

Much gratitude is due from Stamford to the chief agent in gathering so quickly such a company. Few men could have succeeded in enrolling them so soon, and fewer still in organizing and so effectively drilling them. All honor to Colonel Brady, who consented to put himself at their head."

Much credit was also due to the efficient aid given to Col. Brady in raising this company, by his lieutenants, Charles A. Hobby and Marcus Waterbury, both of whom were afterwards to render still more signal service in the field.

An immense concourse of citizens gathered at one o'clock in front of Seely's Hall, for their farewell and benedictions to these citizens of the town. Rev. Walter Mitchell, in prayer commended them to the God of battles, and they started on the campaign, from which some of them were not to return. Our company lists will report their special service for the town they represented.

At the same time, Francis R. Leeds, recently cashier of the Stamford Bank, was authorized to recruit a company. His popularity with our business men, and our young men especially, gave him great advantage. A meeting was held on the 15th, at which the Hon. James C. Loomis, of Bridgeport, Cyrus Northrop, now Professor in Yale College, and Mr. Leeds, addressed the citizens. By the 29th, Mr. Leeds was able to report his company more than full. One hundred and ten of our young men had enrolled themselves under his standard and were waiting for orders.

New and pressing appeals came now, daily, for help. The Seventeenth Connecticut were in need of a Chaplain's tent. Under the appeals of Rev. Mr. Evans, the Stamford citizens promptly subscribed one-half the funds needed for this tent —a part of the funds being the offerings of the children of our schools.

Report reaches us of the arrival of 1,500 Union soldiers disabled, at David's Island, and forthwith our Soldiers' Aid Society, which has already been efficiently at work for a year, in furnishing clothing and other things needful for the health and comfort of our "soldier boys," are all over town, gathering what is most wanted by the poor stricken ones in Hospital; and they not only collect the needed funds and prepare the needed restoratives and cordials for the wounded men, but volunteer their services, also, in personal ministry of attention and care.

On Wednesday, Sept. 3d, 1862, we had a repetition of the scenes of April 28th, 1861. Everybody was out to bid Godspeed to captain Leeds and his fine company of Stamford sons. The captain had already been presented with a beautiful sword, by his friend, James Morsell, Esq. His first lieutenant, Charles H. Brown, had also been taken quite by surprise on the preceding Saturday evening, at an extemporized meeting of his friends. The Hon. M. F. Merritt, their chairman, announced that the friends of the lieutenant had purchased an elegant sword as their tribute to his patriotism, and called upon Jas. H. Olmstead, Esq., to make the presentation. In his brief yet pertinent speech, Mr. Olmstead said: "I call upon you, then, to receive this sword as a free will offering of your friends. Take it as such, and may it be the pen with which you shall write your name upon the pages of your country's history." "Our prayers shall be, that after the tramp of war shall be ended, and our Union again restored, God in his infinite mercy will return you again to the bosom of your friends, not as a lieutenant, but bearing a higher title, well earned and merited by your noble acts while battling for the salvation of your country."

The second lieutenant, Philip Lever, had also been presented with a sword from his friends, and with a seven-shooter, by Mr. Judd of the Phœnix Company. At the same time with the enrollment of Mr. Leeds' company, Cyrus D. Jones, Esq., another of our townsmen, who had just successfully established himself in business on High Ridge, resolved to take part also in the service, and was authorized by the Governor to raise another company.

On the same day which witnessed the departure of captain Leeds' company, a special town meeting was held to provide for the needed quota now due from Stamford. The meeting voted to borrow $10,000, and to give $100 bounty to all who should volunteer for Mr. Jones' company. Daily meetings were now held in the village, at the Turn of the River, and at High and Long Ridges, to fill up the quota. In the meeting called for Wednesday morning Sept. 10th, Wm. H. Holly, Esq., announced that he was authorized by a responsible gentleman to add ten dollars apiece to the bounty of the next ten men who would enlist. Oliver Hoyt added five dollars to the ten just offered, and five more for each additional man who should enlist, and the same for those who had been already sworn in. In the afternoon, Mr. George Elder and Oliver Hoyt pledged themselves to give twenty-five dollars additional bounty to every man in the company.

Among the volunteers who now came forward was Nelson B. Bennet, and his words as well as his example were effective pleas for more volunteers. And so, under these persuasive calls the work of recruiting rapidly advanced. On the 15th of the month the company of Mr. Jones was filled up, and ready for starting for their rendezvous in New Haven.

After a collation at Seely's Hall they were escorted, as the preceding companies had been, to the depot; as was natural the interest of the community had risen, as the pressure of the call from the government increased; so that a larger number of our citizens were present to witness the departure of this last company raised in the town, than at any previous departure.

A singular service for Stamford was held Sunday evening, Sept. 21, 1862, in the Methodist Church of the village. The Sunday School of the church had gathered in special concert to present one of their number, Captain C. D. Jones, with a sword. The presentation was made in an appropriate speech by Oliver Hoyt, Esq., the Superintendent.

While Capt. Leeds' company were still in camp in New Haven, news reached the Governor, then in that city, that there had been riotous opposition to the draft in Fairfield. The Governor promptly detailed Capt. Leeds' company to suppress the riot. The captain happened to be absent from the city when the orders reached the camp, but though the company had then been two hours on drill, under their lieutenants, they started at once for the scene of the riot, corporal Weed rising from a sick bed to join them, thus early showing their readiness for any service to which they might be called.

This was the last company formally raised in the town, though down to the end of the war, men were constantly recruited here. Though once during the war, resort was had to drafting to supply the men we needed, by October, 1864, we had exceeded the demands of the general government. While the three new levies of this year, required 298 men as the quota of Stamford, our loyalty had already furnished 331, giving us a credit of 33 men against any further claims which the government might make.

On Sunday, October 5th, a service, similar to that reported in the Methodist Church, took place in the Baptist Church. The Sunday School of this church had purchased a sword for lieutenant John Simms, one of the teachers of the school. In his modest reply to the presentation speech, made by Mr. Evans, the pastor, he pledged what his friends found to be abundantly fulfilled in the brief service in which he was permitted to wield the sword. "I can only say, that I shall endeavor to merit the good opinion of the donors of this sword, and by God's help it shall never be disgraced."

Early in November, while the Twenty-eighth Regiment, to which both of these companies had been assigned, was still in camp Terry, New Haven, it was hinted by one of our citizens, that as Stamford was so largely represented in the regiment, the colors should be contributed by the citizens. Messrs. James H. Olmstead and Oliver Hoyt secured the needed funds, and on the 15th of the month had the pleasure of presenting the flag in the name of Stamford citizens to the regiment. Mr. Olmstead made the presentation speech. In this address were words to be remembered. " The best and almost the only truly constitutional government of any age, has been ruthlessly assailed, not by a foreign foe, but by those who have grown up under its protection, and who are indebted to it for every civil and religious privilege. * * * You have done nobly in laying yourselves on the altar of your country. * * * To you, then, we entrust these colors, feeling confident that though they may be rent by the iron hail of the battle field, yet they will be brought back by you, or the ground shall be heaped with the slain of those who have dared to dishonor them."

In behalf of the regiment, Col. Ferris, a son of the town, accepted the colors, giving his pledge that " while there is a single strong arm among these sons of Connecticut, this emblem of our nation, and this flag of our State shall never be stained with the pollution of rebel hands."

Special calls upon the town were made several times during the war, by the United States Christian Commission, for the Army and Navy. At a meeting in Seely's Hall, March 18, 1863, after several earnest addresses made for the cause, over eleven hundred dollars were collected. At another meeting, held June 2, 1864, though on a stormy evening, fifteen hundred were promptly pledged. And the whole amount contributed through this channel to the wants of our suffering men in the field, could not have been less than five thousand dollars.

It would be impossible now to report all the service rendered in Stamford, to the cause of the Union, in the shape of clothing, provisions, cordials and hospital stores. Almost every family in the town aided in these contributions. Nothing seemed withheld which could promote the health or comfort of our men in the field. At whatever cost goods were often forwarded to every regiment in which we were more specially represented.

Yet, among the agencies employed in doing this much needed work, especial mention should be made of the SOLDIERS' AID SOCIETY. This was composed of ladies, representing the Congregational, Episcopal, Baptist, Methodist, and Universalist denominations of the village. They organized on the 2d of July 1861, and continued to render good service through the war, reserving, even at its close, such funds as might still be needed for disabled soldiers or their families. In their weekly meetings, and at their private homes, the amount of work they did was very great, and its value can never be fully estimated. As a mere hint at this service, I find that they had forwarded by February, 1862, to our men in the field, 1,288 different articles of clothing, besides medicine and provisions. In the year 1862, they forwarded 642 pairs of socks for one article alone. From July, 1861, to February, 1865, they had collected and made most effective use of the sum of $6,476.18. A considerable portion of this sum had been invested in materials for clothing, which, when made up, must have been of far greater value to our men in the field and in the hospital than a much larger sum of money. Probably $10,000 would not equal the value of the services thus rendered; and this service was the tribute which the great majority of our mothers, and wives, and daughters paid to their loyalty.

The successive presidents of the association were Mrs. Theodore Davenport, Mrs. Truman Smith, Mrs. Mary E. Miller, and Mrs. H. B. Starr; its vice-president, Mrs. E. Francis; its corresponding secretary, Miss C. Tomlinson; its secretaries, Miss Catharine Aiken, and Miss A. Lovell; and its only and very efficient treasurer, Miss Laura E. Porter. The following names are found on its Board of management: Mrs. Ann Ebbets, Mrs. M. F. Merritt, Mrs. G. A. Hoyt, Mrs. J. W. Hubbard, Mrs. James Warner, Mrs. J. H. Carrington, Mrs. R. E. Rice, Mrs. James Betts, Mrs. C. E. Warren, Mrs. J. L. Lockwood, Mrs. Mary E. Miller, Mrs. Woodford, Mrs. C. Weed, Mrs. Caldwell, Mrs. E. Webb, Mrs. William Hoyt, Mrs. Albert Seely, Mrs. H. Weed, Mrs. Dr. Hurlbutt, Mrs. H. M. Humphrey, Mrs. J. B. Knapp, Mrs. William G. Betts, and the Misses Sarah Hall, Susan Daskam, Mary Lockwood, Imogene Macien, and A. Crom.

A very important part of the aid rendered by the Aid Society, consisted in the supplies of provision and cordials for our soldiers at David's Island, and to our wounded men returning to their homes or hospitals through the town. During her presidency, Mrs. Truman Smith, with characteristic resolution, organized a system of regular visitation to the Island, in which a great amount of timely service was rendered by herself and those who accompanied her. The Soldier's Aid Society received many a letter from relieved soldiers, overflowing with heartiest thankfulness for the most excellent work which they were doing so efficiently.

Telegrams from the city often came to the Society, announcing the speedy arrival of a train of cars, having on board a large number of wounded men to be nursed, or a hungry regiment to be fed; and forthwith a detail of Stamford women were on hand at the depot, with the needed supplies.

Such is a part of the work done by the spontaneous liberality of our private citizens—our free-will offerings to a cause in which were centered our highest interests and our best hopes.

But not less noticeable was the public and official action of the town itself. Its recorded votes are a perpetual witness to the earnest loyalty of its citizens. Generous provision was made at the public expense, that the draft which had been ordered, need not bear unjustly upon those of our townsmen who might be unable to meet the expense of substitutes. Witness the vote of August 4, 1863, in which a bounty of $300 was provided for every drafted man who should be accepted by the Government. Without reporting each appropriation made, as the exigency of the war called for it, it is only necessary to add, as a witness to the generous provision of the town, that our treasury shows, between April, 1861, and October 11, 1865, appropriations for war purposes to the amount of $75,627.85.

We have thus briefly gathered some of the proofs of the loyal zeal shown by the citizens of Stamford, during these months and years of the great Secession experiment. Such zeal and such sacrifice could only have sprung from an abiding love for the Union of the States, and from strong convictions that there is no safety nor even a continued history for us, without such union. At the opening of the war, it was as if a whole people, moved by the sense of a common peril, had united with all their resources to effect their common deliverance. Nor, at any time during the war, did any other opposition to the war measures show itself, than such as simply served to re-invigorate, and show in still clearer light the anti-secession element in the town.

CITIZEN SERVICE. 31

Among the most effective means by which these results were secured we must not lose sight of the teachings and the examples of our pulpits. As in revolutionary times of old, the clergy of the town were, in loyal zeal and works, the leaders and examples to their people. During the few months preceding actual collision, there were earnest pleas for peace, and earnest prayer that if it could be, civil war might be averted. At our Union services on the occasion of the fast appointed by president Buchanan, it seemed as though the shrinking back from the threatened conflict, foreboded a future timidity which could never face the hazards of actual war. But when the war note had been once sounded, in spite of this hope of peace, and prayer for it, no pulpit here which spoke at all, gave an uncertain sound. "Political preaching," as never before, summoned the worshipers of these churches to an earnest and self-sacrificing loyalty. The calls of the government were enforced in sacred places, as the very call of God. Treason was pronounced impiety; and so religion was held to be inseparable from patriotism. In the Baptist church, the Rev. P. S. Evans, lost no opportunity to urge upon the people the grave duty of the hour. No day was too holy, in his creed, and no place too sacred, for the utterance and the enforcement of loyalty, and he never stopped to apologize for either; and when the time came for him to show his faith by his works, he was found ready to take his place as chaplain in the army, with his regiment at the front.

Rev. R. R. Booth, of the Presbyterian church, who left his charge here just as the assassins of the nation were concerting the methods of their attack, in his parting words, left behind him the germs of right thoughts for the coming crisis; and his successor, Rev. D. K. Bartlett, poured into the work here, all the warmth and earnestness of a passion for loyalty and a righteous indignation against treason; and went, like Mr. Evans, with his regiment, to do the service of an Army Chaplain.

Rev. L. S. Weed of the Methodist church remained here long enough to see the people earnestly at work in the strife, and his weighty words had their influence in rallying our strength to the standard of the Union; and both his successors, Drs. Burch and Andrews, only seconded and sustained the loyalty, which he enforced.

Rev. L. W. Bacon, of the Congregational church, gave us his clear and sharp analysis of treason; and by an eloquence not often exceeded, stirred the people to whatever duty, of patient forbearance or courageous warfare, a Christian patriotism demanded of them.

Rev. Walter Mitchell, of the Episcopal church, both in his own pulpit and in the mass meetings of our citizens—in discourse and in verse, earnestly enjoined on all good citizens the sacred duties of citizenship in the crisis which had come.

Rev. Eben Francis, in the Universalist church, held the same theory of loyalty with our other clergy, and in many a timely and eloquent word, spoke nobly for the cause. He rendered, also, effective service in the chaplaincy which he so well filled. Nor was his co-laborer and successor, Rev. J. S. Dodge, a whit behind the foremost of these loyal ministers, in either the doctrine or practice of his loyalty.

It is due, also, to the memory of Father O'Neil of the Catholic church, to add, that, being a republican, he was in full sympathy with the prosecution of the war, though in his feeble state, unable to give it an active and public advocacy.

It should also be added, that in addition to the chaplain services of at least three of these ministers, others of them rendered very effective aid to our cause in their voluntary agency for the United States Christian and Sanitary Commissions.

Under such teachings, appealing as they did to the responsive hearts of a loyal people, and enforced as they were, by almost daily examples of such practical and self-denying devotion to the cause, as never fails to move human hearts, it is not to be wondered at, that at times, this zeal for the Union cause seemed to be excessive. Warm-hearted men would be very likely to assume risks and responsibilities, greater even than the cause could ask at their hands. Young men, eager to avenge an insult offered for the first time in their lives to their country's flag, even if without the physical endurance needed for the field, would be very likely to crowd forward, even over the wishes of their friends and the warnings of the surgeon, to a place with the most valiant in the ranks.

We are not without many instances, in which the sons of the town were kept out of the ranks, only by the refusal of the surgeon to allow the muster. We could wish it possible to enroll here, in our record of CITIZEN SERVICE, the free-will offerings which they thus made. But their names were never recorded on the muster roll, and many of them were never reported outside of the families which they represented. We recall only these few as the representatives of this class of our young loyalists:—Charles W., son of Rufus Wardwell; Arthur W., son of Charles Edwin Smith; Augustus, son of Sanford Bates; and George, son of Wm. Dayton.

Others among us, whose years exempted them, sought to show their zeal, side by side with their sons in the field; and our ranks thus actually held men whose years would have been a bar to their enlistment.

Others, still, who were personally exempt, outstripped

the letter of their duty, by furnishing an extra and reserve soldier, who might possibly be needed in some special emergency, or who might save the stern necessity of calling away from the support of his dependent family, one whom the law of the war called to a sacrifice which he ought not to be required to make. How long this list should be we may never know; but to their honor and our credit, we may here record upon it the names of Captain William Skiddy and Alfred Hoyt, Esq., of whom Captain Skiddy sent a soldier for himself, though above the military age, and his son who had not yet attained it.

To this list it is due that at least one other name should be added, J. N. Ayres, Esq. When, by the sad fortune of the war, he had been called to lay his own son in a soldier's grave, he did not rest, until he had refilled by a substitute, at his own cost, the vacancy thus made in the ranks.

And then what a record we have in the gift to the country, in this hour of her great peril, of so many of the sons from so many of our families. Our catalogue will show us one family offering eight of its sons and grandsons; another lending the services of six sons, of whom one, wrecked by the storms of war, returned only to linger on till his death; three others gave for us five sons each, four others four sons each, and eleven others still, each three sons. We have not yet counted up the families from which both father and son went, side by side into the war; nor those which sent two sons each; nor yet those from which the only son went, never more to return; nor those whose fathers, bidding their wives and little ones tearful adieus, heroically went forth facing the perils of the field, to return in so many instances no more, to the home-hearths they offered themselves to save. We do not attempt to chronicle here the story of home-ties sundered, and home-affections torn, and home-hopes forever blighted in these years of war. This is the story that pen cannot trace. It is felt, only, in the tearless and voiceless depths of anguished and patiently suffering souls. And we had them here, aye, and now have them among us. Oh! how many of them.

More than any other of these varied services, will the great sacrifice of life among us, remain an unequivocal witness to the fealty of the people. No town, for any trivial cause, would consent to such a sacrifice. There must be rights unspeakably costly and precious, in danger; or the very principles on which all those rights depend, must be at stake, before a people will pay such a cost. How much we had thus suffered in our family circles was seen with painful distinctness as the Thanksgiving of 1864 approached. It was proposed to send the Thanksgiving Turkey to every widow whose husband had fallen in the war, when the following list was supplied: Mrs. G. W. Platt, J. Waters, S. H. Hoyt, J. A. Miles, Geo. C. Swathel, F. Bryson, J. J. Taylor, H. Mahan, M. Fox, W. Gillespie, C. E. Morrell, L. L. Hoyt, E. B. Bouton, J. Vail, A. J. Lockwood, S. D. Lockwood, W. O. Webb, G. A. Mead, A. Boyd, T. O'Brien, T. L. Bailey, N. Barmore, P. Fryermouth, A. Hoyt, G. W. Hartson, C. Jennings, C. W. Miller, S. Smith and Wm. H. Walton. How much more the town was to suffer in this sacrifice of life, our too long roll of the dead, at the close of this volume will show. But the record—full as it is—and representing as it does all classes of families among us, will prove to us a most enduring witness to the deep and unconquerable loyalty of a people, who were ready to pledge the last dollar and the last man, to resist the wicked counsels and the wily assaults of treason.

And yet, why need we marvel even at such exhibitions of a self-denying and self-sacrificing loyalty? What have not a people been willing to do and dare in other years and in other lands, in self-defense? What are the bounds, beyond which earnestly loyal souls will not venture, for the sake of father-land and fealty?

Nay, it would have been a greater marvel, if when rebel shots first struck the Nation's Sumpter, a single citizen could be found, outside of the conspirators themselves, whose honest fear and hottest indignation did not rouse him to a hero's part in the defense. It would have been a marvel, if Stamford had not poured out her money and her men to meet and crush out, quickly and forever, this fell germ of treason. Yes, thank God, it is his ordinance. HE gives to loyalty the enthusiasm which knows no bounds. He inspires stout hearts, he nerves strong arms to do his work, when treason assails his cause. And when thus inspired and nerved, why should not the hosts of loyalty triumph? Why should not "the right hand of the Lord" be exalted?

"THE RIGHT HAND OF THE LORD DOETH VALIANTLY."

PART SECOND.

MILITARY SERVICE.

MILITARY SERVICE.

In this portion of the MEMORIAL we shall report as fully as our space will allow, the position and service of every native or resident of the town, who has been in any way connected with the army, or with the navy of the Union. And every name on our roll will appear in its appropriate place in the company, or regiment, or battalion, to which it properly belongs. As the town was much more fully represented in the Third, Sixth, Tenth, Seventeenth and Twenty-eighth regiments of Connecticut volunteers, than in any others, we shall first report these regiments with a list of their principal engagements, as the most intelligible and briefest way of locating the great majority of our townsmen in the war.

To these will succeed the list of our townsmen scattered through the other regiments of the State, with such personal notices as we can supply. Then will follow our representatives in the regiments of other States, alphabetically arranged; and the last list will be that of those who have been in the regular service in the United States army.

For the Connecticut portion of this list, I am not a little indebted to the "Catalogue of the Connecticut Volunteer Force" issued by the Adjutant General of the State, though my list will differ considerably from that of the State catalogue, both in the number of the names and in their orthography. For the list of names connected with the regiments of other States, I have been obliged to depend mainly upon my own private record of our townsmen, as from week to week during the struggle, their enlistment came to my knowledge. The lists secured from both of these sources have been considerably modified by personal application to more than a hundred and fifty of these volunteers or their families. If errors are still found in the list, or if omissions are detected, they must be such as have occurred in spite of the most laborious and expensive pains-taking.

At the head of each of these fuller companies, will be indicated the times of mustering in, of re-enlistment, and of final discharge, so that these facts need not be repeated at each name. When, in individual cases, enlistment or discharge occurred at other times, the record will be found against the names to which they refer.

THIRD CONN.

Colonels John Arnold, and J. L. Chatfield.

In this Regiment, Company F, Stamford was represented by thirty-nine men. Their captain, Albert Stevens, on the opening of the war, was residing in the town, and having already seen considerable service, and being thoroughly in sympathy with the aim of the war, he was commissioned to be their leader. The balance of the company consisted of eighteen men from Darien and thirteen from New Canaan.

Leaving Stamford Monday morning, April 18, 1861, the company went to their rendezvous in Hartford, where they were set earnestly to the work of fitting themselves for the field. Scarcely a man of them ever handled fire-arms, least of all with any design of putting them to a military use. Of the spirit of these men we had a good illustration in an incident occurring while they were on drill in Hartford, before they were mustered. They had been encouraged before leaving home with the promise of equipment with Sharp's rifles. Instead of these, notice came to them that they would have to march with the old smooth-bore musket. They were, of course, tried by the disappointment, and protested against the order. But the times allowed of no delay; and when the captain called upon those in the ranks, who would go on with him to meet the enemy, even if the Government would give them "nothing but pitchforks," to step forward, every man of them sprang to the front. And this was the spirit which animated them to the end of the term for which they had enlisted, and which led so many of them to re-enlist. They were at length mustered into the service in Hartford, for three months, leaving that city, May 19th, for New Haven, where they took the steamer Cahawba for Washington. Here they joined, May 23d, the First and Second Connecticut Regiments, and were put under vigorous drill in camp Douglas, until June 23d, when they were ordered to camp Tyler, at Falls Church, in Virginia, and for several days they held this exposed position. On a scouting expedition to Hunter's Road, June 30th, Captain Stevens, with forty of his command, took three horses and two prisoners from the famed Black Horse Cavalry of the rebels. One of the horses thus taken was used by General Tyler on the day of the Bull Run rout.

On July 15th, our three Connecticut Regiments were brigaded with the Eleventh Maine, under Col. E. D. Keyes, and on the next day were ordered to advance, the Third Connecticut taking the lead. They were arrested at Blackburn Ford, by Longstreet's division; and here for two days of varied skirmishing, the brigade held this advanced post, while the Union forces were brought up. We next find our company entering the apparently disastrous Bull Run engagement, July 21, 1861. We shall never know all of the daring of those terrible hours. Terry was ordered at about two o'clock P. M. to take a battery, which greatly annoyed the Union troops. It was while executing this order that our company showed itself ready for the severest ordeals of war. Meeting, they drove before them the skirmish lines of the enemy to the very summit of the hill, over which the batteries were masked and supported by infantry, and there, " unfurled the stars and stripes above it, pausing from the fight to cheer for the Union cause."

Among the men who represented us on that day, must be named as especially deserving mention, our first and second lieutenants, Wells Allis and Isaac L. Hoyt, and our First Sergeant, Charles A. Hobbie. It was well earned testimony which General Keyes was obliged to render this regiment in his official report, and to no part of his command did it more truthfully apply, than to our Stamford representatives:— " The gallantry with which the Second regiment of Maine and the Third of Connecticut Volunteers, charged up the hill upon the enemy's artillery and infantry was never, in my opinion, surpassed." No higher praise is needed for these sons of the town, than that being first in the engagements of that unfortunate day, they were also the last to leave the field ; and that they left it, not like the great mass of the Union army, in a disgraceful rout, but in good order, and with their arms. To this record we can also add, that by hard fighting, they had to defend themselves and protect for several miles the retreating army. We have, also, Gen. Tyler's testimony, that it was the good conduct of these sons of Connecticut, which "saved us, not only a large amount of public property, but the mortification of having our standing camps fall into the hands of the enemy." Our company roll at the end of this account mentions the capture of three of our men: It is due to one of these prisoners of war, that we here give the story of his capture. George Weed, the third on the list of those taken prisoners, had been assisting Robert Wilson and Charles Hunnewell of our company, and A. E. Bronson of Co. C, in removing from the hospital, Sergeant John R. Marsh of Danbury, who was in a dying condition. The agony of the wounded soldier was such that he begged them to take him up into a piece of woods near them, and let him die. They did so, and there watched over him, with such ministry of kindness as they could render, until his death.* This had taken so much time, as to make it difficult for them to overtake their regiment, then on the retreat ; and none of them succeeded in eluding the pursuing army, excepting the shrewd and active Wilson. And so, devotion to his wounded comrade cost Mr. Weed his capture and imprisonment. The company after the rout at Bull Run were not again called into the field. Returning to Connecticut at the expiration of the three months for which they had enlisted, they were mustered out with the regiment at Hartford. On their return to Stamford, they were welcomed in a brief address of congratulation on behalf of their townsmen, by the author of this MEMORIAL, and with a prayer of thanksgiving by Rev. L. S. Weed, of the Methodist church. The response, made by Capt. Stevens, to the address, indicated the readiness of the company to re-enter service, as soon as they could recover from the wear of their past three months' campaign. The following catalogue will show who of them re-enlisted ; and the records of the companies which they joined, will witness to the good service that many of them did, as proved and accredited VETERANS.

---

* This record will correct an error which crept into the note on page 100 of the excellent " Military and Civil History of Connecticut during the Civil War."

RIFLE COMPANY F.

Mustered into the United States Service, May 14, 1861. Mustered out August 12, 1861.

ALBERT STEVENS, Capt., re-enl. into the 17th Conn.
WELLS ALLIS, 1st Lieut., re-enl. into the 95th Ohio.
THEODORE MILLER, Sergt., re-enl. into the 10th Conn.
EDWARD F. NICHOLS, Sergt., afterwards served in the Navy.
MARCUS WATERBURY, Sergt., re-enl. into the 17th Conn.
HENRY M. CAPPER, Corp., re-enl. into the 10th Conn.
JACOB VANDERHOFF, Corp., re-enl. into 17th Conn.
THADDEUS L. BAILEY, Corp., re-enl. into the 28th Conn.
PHILIP LEVEE, Musician, re-enl. into the 28th Conn.
JOHN H. VERNAL, Musician, re-enl. into the 17th Conn.
SMITH BROWN, was discharged for disability.
ELA BALLARD, re-enl. into the 28th Conn.
EDSON BEARDSLEY, re-enl. into the 17th Conn.
CHARLES A. BAILEY, did not re-enlist.
EDWARD J. BING, Jr., re-enl. into the 6th Conn.
JAMES CONLAN, re-enl. into the 8th Conn.
CHARLES I. DAYTON, entered the Navy.
THEODORE DELCROIX, re-enl. into the 28th Conn.
EDWARD A. FERRIS, re-enl. into the 28th Conn.
JOSHUA D. GILMORE, taken prisoner at Bull Run, July 21, 1861, and held as a prisoner until the next spring, re-enl. into some foreign regiment.
WILLIAM HOBBIE. See Obituary.
JOHN HARVEY, re-enl. into the 17th Conn.
CHARLES H. KELIG, re-enl. into the 6th Conn.
JOHN KELLEY, is not known to have re-enlisted.
JOHN KELLY, 2d, re-enl. into the 17th Conn.
HENRY I. LOUNSBURY, re-enl. into the 17th Conn.
MICHAEL MURPHY, is not known to have re-enlisted.
JOSEPH PAIGHT, taken prisoner at Bull Run, July 21, 1861, and held by the rebels eleven months. After his release, he re-enl. into the 28th Conn.

MILITARY SERVICE.—CO. F, THIRD CONN.   45

Peter Rooney, it is thought, went into a New York cavalry regiment.
George A. Scofield, re-enl. into the 17th Conn.
David H. Scofield, re-enl. into the Ira Harris cavalry.
James T. Scofield, re-enl. into 17th Conn.
John Simms, re-enl. into the 10th Conn.
Theodore W. Swan, returned to his business here.
Francis L. Still, re-enl. in the 6th Conn.
Alonzo P. Toms, returned to his business here.
Orlando Townsend, re-enl. into the 6th Conn.
James E. Webb, discharged for disability; is now living in Peekskill, N. Y.
George Weed, was taken prisoner at Bull Run, July 21, 1861. He was exchanged in July, 1862, and re-enl. into the 17th Conn.

SIXTH CONN.

Cols. J. L. Chatfield, D. C. Rodman, Redfield Duryee, and A. P. Rockwell.

In company D of this regiment, Stamford was represented, before the close of the war by 107 men. As a regiment it took rank among the most efficient; and none of its companies did better service than the Stamford company. This was distinctly foretokened, both by the character of the volunteers themselves, and still more by the special military fitness of their captain. We were not surprised to have the company thus reported by an intelligent correspondent from New Haven while they were still in camp there: "This company is admitted by all to be the best company on the ground. Even captains of other companies concede this much. The men have been longer and better drilled. Out of 84 men only two were rejected. Altogether, Stamford has cause to be proud of the company, and I am satisfied it will never disgrace your citizens."

Nor was it altogether an unexpected award made to the regiment, later in the war, by its Brigadier, Horatio G. Wright: " The Sixth is my best regiment—they have done more work, taken more property, and behaved better, than any other of my regiments."

This regiment left New Haven, Sept. 17th, 1861, and at Jersey City took cars for Washington. After remaining in tents at Glenwood until Oct. 5th, they went to Annapolis, where they embarked, Oct. 20th with sixteen other regiments, for the expedition to South Carolina under Sherman; and on the 29th they left Fortress Monroe, to begin in earnest the severe work to which they were called. After the successful naval action of Nov. 7th, in which Forts Walker and Beauregard were taken, the honor was assigned to the Sixth and Seventh Connecticut regiments of first landing on rebel territory, and taking possession of it in the name of the government of the United States. The Sixth, in command of captain Meeker, on board the Winfield Scott, and the Seventh under Col. Terry in row boats, started together, to execute this order. The steamer grounding just off Fort Walker, the opportunity is afforded to the row boats to reach the shore first, and the Seventh rapidly formed on the beach, while the Sixth were landing; and Hilton Head was now in the hands of the Union forces.

Under date of Nov. 29th we have the following account of the first permanent occupancy of the main land by our army, in a letter from captain Meeker:

" Last Saturday morning, we left Hilton Head and the same day reached Graham's Plantation. On Sunday morning, Nov. 24th, we started for Buckingham Ferry. As we approached the shore, we discovered some eight or ten of the enemy's pickets, on whom we fired at once. They immediately mounted their horses and fled like deer. * * The men behaved nobly and landed from the boats in fine style. Without the least hesitation they leaped into the water, where it was three or four feet deep and rushing to the shore formed in good order. This was the first expedition to the main land, except when I crossed some eight days before with nine men.

On Monday, John Vandervaldt, Martin Stottlar, Bob Wilson and Scriber went on an expedition of their own to the main land. They drove in the secesh pickets— took their flag and brought it into camp, the only one taken except the one on the fort at the time of bombardment."

It would have amused us to see our energetic captain attempt the exploration of Seceshdom on a secesh mule. He had gone over to Bull Island, on a military errand. Obliged to leave his own horse in camp, he found the need of one on the island. He soon spied a negro driving his mule in his cart; and on learning from him that the beast was good under the saddle, he negotiated for his use. He mounted and started with his company, but his vicious donkey used his heels so skilfully as to leave his rider at his leisure on the sward, while his donkeyship careered at 2.40 speed around the fields.

The early part of 1862 found this company still in the Department of the South. For more than a month they were on board transports in Warsaw Sound, to be ready at a signal to take part in a secret expedition, headed by Gen. Wright. Nothing could exceed their discomfort during this trying period. Salt food only, and foul water, with their crowded transports, left them a prey to the fever of the region, and they were obliged to return to Hilton Head, where they rapidly recovered. In March they were sent over to Dawfuskie Island, to take part in the reduction of Fort Pulaski. In May they are ordered to James' Island, near Charleston, and in executing this order our men saw not a little privation. Returning to Hilton Head, they remained until October 21st, when they were sent on an expedition to break up railroad communication between Charleston and Savannah. The pilot of this raid was one of our men, Robert Wilson. On the 22d occurred the sharp fighting at Pocataligo, in which our company dared well, and suffered much as skirmishers, under lieutenant J. Stottlar; the captain being in command of the regiment after the fall of the colonel and his lieutenant-colonel, John Speidal.

The winter of 1862-3 was spent in camp at Beaufort and Hilton Head. In March, 1863, they were in Florida, but after evacuating Jacksonville, returned to Hilton Head. Early in June, 1863, the company were transferred to Folly Island, where for nearly a month they were quietly engaged in making preparations for taking possession of Morris Island, lying between them and Charleston. No night succeeded which did not tax to the utmost their skill and their endurance; and by the 9th of July they had made ready for the advance. Here our men did most effective service. As the regiment under their gallant colonel landed, Company D were ordered to deploy as skirmishers to the front. Under their first and second lieutenants, John and Martin Stottlar, they started at "double quick," mounted the first battery and captured all the gunners, and sent them to the rear as prisoners of war. They then filed off to the left, mounting the second battery as the first, and so on until all the batteries were carried, numbering in all twelve batteries of siege guns. The color-bearer of the rebels was making off with their battle flag, when Roper Hounslow shot him down. Lieutenant Martin Stottlar being close at his heels, took the flag the moment he fell. It bore the date which our boys could never have forgotten, Pocotaligo, October 22, 1862. The batteries had been taken in fine style, Company D alone taking sixty-four prisoners, when its whole number of effective men was but sixty-two.

Again, after a night of furious rain in the rifle pits, the company joined with a will in the severe charge on Wagner, of the 18th. The first Lieut. John Stottlar, was sent to the front with the body of his command as sharpshooters, and the thirteen who were not in the pits, were in the furious charge which followed, under their second Lieut., Martin Stottlar. How desperate was the work which our men here did, is seen in the fact that before the colors of the Sixth Conn. were planted on the fort, eleven color-bearers had been shot down. And what was worse than the perilous advance on Wagner and the storming of its well-worked batteries, amid the shot and shell which the Sumpter and James' Island batteries were pouring upon the advancing column, was the courageous feat of holding the fort alone for three hours, against three desperate attempts of the rebels to recover it.

Among the men who were counted worthy of special remembrance and honor for the daring work of this fierce fighting, our company counts two, to whom General Gilmore awarded medals of honor, Sergeant Norman Provost and Horace Hobby.

The Sixth, after the severe work they had done before Wagner, were sent back to Hilton Head for recruiting. In January, 1864, they had a short furlough, during which they visited the North, and were welcomed at New Haven by a midnight exhibition of fireworks and a sumptuous supper. A complimentary supper was also given the re-enlisted men

of this company, February 20, 1864, at the Stamford
House, when their captain, Charles H. Nichols, was presented with a sword from the citizens of Stamford, by Thos.
G. Ritch, Esq. J. B. Ferris, Esq., followed the presentation
by handing to the captain a purse containing $1050, to be
distributed equally among the forty-two re-enlisted men.

Returning South, they embarked April 6th, at Hilton
Head, and proceeded to Gloucester Point in Virginia, where
they were assigned to the 10th Army Corps, under Major-
Gen. Gilmore. May 4th, they embarked on transports and
proceeded up the James' river, and by the 10th, we find the
Sixth, now led by our townsman, lieutenant-colonel Meeker,
doing good service, near Chester Station, destroying the
track of the Richmond and Petersburg railroad.

From this date until the 16th, our men were almost constantly engaged in skirmishing, until they felt, on the morning of the latter date, the sudden and heavy fall of the rebel
army upon their exposed front before Fort Darling. During
these days of constant exposure, nine of the Stamford men
were more or less severely wounded, as the company roll
will show. May 20th witnessed another engagement in
which they succeeded in capturing a portion of the advanced
rifle pits of the rebels, when two more of our townsmen are
reported among the wounded. Next followed the engagement of June 17th, near Bermuda Hundred. This time
Longstreet pounced upon our advance with a heavy force,
and captured Captain Nichols and nine of his command, and,
of course, gave them a trial of the tender mercies of rebel
prison life, as they had occasion to learn on reaching Libby
the next evening. "Here," and we are following the captain's own diary, "we were searched by the notorious Dick
Turner, and I had all my greenbacks taken from me. On
the morning of the 19th, about ten o'clock, our rations for

the day were brought in ; they were one-half pint of cow pea soup, two ounces rotten bacon, and one half pound corn bread."

Thence on the 21st they were sent to Macon, Ga., where, on the following Fourth of July, they raised the stars and stripes, " much to the disgust of the officers " in charge of them. July 28th they were sent to Charleston, and thence, October 5th, to Columbia, and assigned quarters in an open field without shelter. November 4th, the captain escaped, and after a tramp of ninety miles was captured November 9th, and sent back to Columbia. On the 29th he made his escape again with several others. The captain's diary shall explain how he this time succeeded.

" Before going to our hiding place at daylight, we called on the negroes who had helped us on our previous journey. One of them told us that the dogs would be run that day, but we could fool the dogs. So we were led to the barn and put in the hay loft, where we lay all day and the next night, the negroes cooking rations for us and bringing them to us. THE NEGROES WERE TRUE TO US IN EVERY INSTANCE. After leaving this place, we found other negroes who helped us in every way they could. After traveling at night and lying still in the day, for ten days, we arrived safely at the coast, and were rescued by the picket boat from the United States gun boat, Nipsic." As it happened, his deliverer was another of our townsmen, engineer L. L. P. Ayres. After being thus rescued, the captain was sent to Charleston harbor, where he reported to the fleet commander, and was sent to Port Royal. From Port Royal he went to New York, which he reached December 20, 1864.

Meanwhile, in the engagements at Deep Run, from the 14th to the 18th of August, our men again saw hard fighting and sustained some losses—captain John Stottlar and eight of his command being the victims of these incessant skirmishes. From this date forward, whether at the front, steadily facing Richmond—the real seat of the rebel power—or before New York—threatened with a mild form of rebellion from the foreign population, our company continued to merit well for brave and honorable service. And when Terry had obtained permission to take Fort Fisher, he turned to our Sixth and Seventh regiments, whose gallant service he had so often witnessed, to share with him the brilliant achievement which made that "impregnable" fort our own, and the subsequent movement which opened Wilmington to our troops.

The report of the Adjutant-General of the State for 1866, gives the following as the principal engagements in which this regiment took part:—Pocotaligo, October 22, 1862; Morris Island, July 10, 1863; Fort Wagner, July 18, 1863; all in South Carolina; Chester Station, May 10, 1864; Near Bermuda Hundred, May 10 to June 18, 1864, Deep Run, August 14 to 18, 1864, in Virginia; and Fort Fisher, N. C., January 15, 1865.

COMPANY D.

This Company was mustered in September 5, 1861, re-enlisted December 24, 1863, and mustered out August 21, 1865.

LORENZO MEEKER, commissioned Capt. August 23d, 1861, promoted Major July 24th, 1862, and Lieut. Col. Nov. 27th, 1863. At the close of his term of service he was urged to remain in the service, in consideration of his efficient conduct in command. He at length resigned, Sept. 30th, 1864, and was honorably discharged.

CHARLES H. NICHOLS, commissioned 1st Lieut. August 23d, 1861, and Capt. July 24th, 1862. An excellent officer in the care of his command and in his steady courage in action. He was detailed in 1861 to organize a guard by Gen. W. T. Sherman, and served also as aid to Col. Chatfield while on James' Island. At Beaufort he rendered good service as Provost Marshal.

JOHN STOTTLAR, commissioned 2d Lieut. August 23, 1861, promoted 1st Lieut. July 24, 1862, and Capt. Feb. 19, 1864, and assigned to Co. C of the regiment. His promotion was the fitting reward for soldierly merit. When needed, he was ready both to dare and to do. At the expiration of his term of enlistment he was honorably discharged Dec. 2, 1864.

WILLIAM H. MEEKER, entered the service as 1st Sergt., and was commissioned 2d Lieut. July 24, 1862. He resigned Feb. 10, 1863.

MARTIN STOTTLAR entered the service, 2d Sergt., was commissioned 2d Lieut. Feb. 10, 1863 and 1st Lieut. Jan. 19, 1864. He deserves well of his townsmen both for his daring on the field and for the patience and courage with which he endured the long suffering, which followed the severe wounds of July 18, 1863, before Fort Wagner. He had well earned the sword presented him by the citizens of the town, in January, 1864. He resigned, March 17, 1864.

NORMAN PROVOST, entered the service as 3d Sergt. He re-enlisted veteran, and was commissioned 2d Lieut. March 17, 1864, and promoted 1st Lieut. May 31, 1864. He brought back with him the medal which testifies to his good conduct on the battle-field.

JOHN H. BOTTS entered the service as private, re-enlisted veteran, and was wounded in the eyes at Bermuda Hundred. He was commissioned 1st Lieut. March 3, 1865, assigned to Co. C., and mustered out with the company.

JOHN VANDERVALT, Sergt., served in the signal corps, and at the end of his term of enlistment was mustered out.

HORACE P. HOBBY, Sergt., re-enl. veteran. See Obituary.

GILES CAREY, Sergt., was discharged for disability in 1863.

GEORGE W. FINCH, Sergt., wounded in hand and hip at Fort Darling, May 20, 1864.
ROBERT WILSON, Corp., an active and useful soldier, wounded in the shoulder at Pocotaligo, and transferred to Inv. Corps Sept. 30, 1863.
THOMAS SCRIBER, Corp., wounded at Fort Darling, May 15, 1864.
GEORGE W. YOUNGS, Corp., detailed for Quartermaster's department.
WM. H. INNESS, Corp., was discharged for disability, Jan. 7, 1863.
EDWARD J. BING, Corp.   See Obituary.
JOEL M. ANDERSON, Corp., re-enl. veteran, and was wounded May 20, 1864. Sent to the hospital in Newark, N. J., and discharged by reason of his wounds, June 28, 1864.
JOHN S. CLARK, Corp., re-enl. veteran.   See Obituary.
CHARLES E. PROVOST, Corp., re-enl. veteran. See Obituary.
WILLIAM LOWA, Corp.   See Obituary.
JAMES MCGEE, Corp., re-enl. veteran on the Stamford quota, and was wounded on Morris Island, July 9, 1863.
IRA D. JONES, Corp., Jan. 30, 1862.   See Obituary.
WM. H. REYNOLDS, Corp., re-enl. veteran on the Stamford quota.
GEORGE LORD, Musician.
CHARLES H. LOCKWOOD, Musician, was trans. Inv. Corps, July 1, 1863.
FREDERICK BATES, Wagoner, re-enl. veteran, Jan. 4, 1864.
GEORGE W. ANDERSON, re-enl. veteran, and discharged by President's Proclamation.
EDWARD ARENTS, was trans. to Inv. Corps Sept. 1, 1863.
SETH S. BOUTON, re-enl. and was captured June 17, 1864.
JOHN BOHAN, was discharged for disability May 24, 1863, and re-enl. Co. I, 10th Conn.
FRANK BRYSON, re-enl. veteran.   See Obituary.
DENNIS BURNS, was wounded at Pocotaligo and trans. to Inv. Corps.

John Clark, re-enl. veteran.
William H. Coyne, re-enl. veteran and reported as deserting April 16, 1864.
Albert W. Crocker, was wounded at Pocotaligo in the foot and re-enl. veteran with the company.
Thomas Craw, re-enl. veteran.
Alonzo Dixon, re-enl. veteran.
John Drew, re-enl. veteran.
David Finch, was trans. to Inv. Corps, Sept. 1, 1863.
Charles E. Finch, re-enl. veteran.
Daniel Freeman.   See Obituary.
John Grady, was wounded severely in the hand at Fort Wagner, July 18, 1863.
John F. Hassenat, living in Greenwich, re-enl. veteran from Stamford, was taken prisoner and escaped.
Roper Hounslow, re-enl. veteran.
George Hoyt, was honorably discharged at the end of his term of enlistment, Sept. 11, 1864.
Henry W. Hoyt.   See Obituary.
John L. Hoyt, was discharged to re-enl. into the U. S. army.
James H. Jerman, enlisted Sept. 6, 1862, and after being on detailed service at Fort Trumbull, Conn., and elsewhere, joined his regiment in May, 1865.
James Jones, re-enl. veteran.
Joseph Jones.   See Obituary.
George W. Kent, was discharged for disability April 29, 1863.
James L. Lockwood, re-enl. veteran.   See Obituary.
Lewis Lower, re-enl. veteran.
Robert McDonald, re-enl. veteran, and was taken prisoner near Bermuda Hundred, and was sent to Andersonville and other rebel prisons. He was paroled Dec. 13, 1864.
John A. Miles.   See Obituary.
Michael Morgan, re-enl. vet. Had one arm broken at Morris Island, and was honorably disch. Sept. 11, 1864.

WILLIAM A. MOREHOUSE. See Obituary.
SILAS NORTHRUP, re-enl. veteran, and was wounded in the shoulder.
FRANK O'BRIEN, re-enl. veteran, wounded May 15, 1864.
WM. S. PEATT, re-enl. veteran. See Obituary.
THOMAS PICKER, re-enl. vet., and taken prisoner June 17, 1864.
PATSY PICKER, enl. Sept. 19, 1862. See Obituary.
JAMES A. POTTS, re-enl. veteran.
EDGAR L. PRATT, re-enl. veteran, Jan. 4, 1863, and wounded May 15, 1864.
ANDREW PROVOST, wounded at Pocotaligo in the arm, and hon. disch. May 28, 1863.
HENRY SCOFIELD re-enl. veteran, and was wounded May 20, 1864, in one knee, and again at Deep Run the following August.
SMITH SCOFIELD wounded at Pocotaligo, and again May 16, 1864, near Bermuda Hundred, and was four months in hospital.
EDWARD SEARLES, re-enl. veteran, and was wounded May 10, 1864 in left hand.
GEORGE E. SEARLES, re-enl. veteran and taken prisoner June 17, 1864, and sent south.
EDWARD M. SEELY. See Obituary.
IRVING L. SNIFFIN, re-enl. veteran on the Stamford quota with the company.
JOHN S. SPARKS, was disch. for disability April 22, 1863.
GEORGE C. SWATHAL, re-enl. veteran. See Obituary.
OSCAR E. SNYDER, re-enl. veteran on the Stamford quota.
BARNEY TONAR, re-enl. vet. was taken prisoner June 17, 1864.
MARINUS W. THORN, re-enl. veteran. See Obituary.
JOSEPH A TOEPFER re-enl. veteran on the Stamford quota.
OLIVER W. VERNAL re-enl. veteran, and was twice wounded.
CHARLES C. WALTERS, re-enl. vet.
EDWARD H. WALTERS re-enl. vet., and transferred to Inv.

Res. Corps., March 15, 1864. He was honorably discharged in October, 1865.

JOHN D. WARD, re-enl. veteran on the Stamford quota.

CHARLES H. WEED, re-enl. vet., Jan. 4, 1864, and was wounded at Pocotaligo, and again in one arm, May 10, 1864.

JOHN A. YOUNGS was detailed, on reaching the South, as captain of a squad of carpenters. He rendered good service to the cause here, by his account of the hardships of our soldiers, while on shipboard and in the swamps of South Carolina. He was discharged for disability, May 24, 1863.

RECRUITS.

JAMES WRIGHT, Co. B, enlisted Sept. 12, 1861, and was discharged to enlist into the U. S. Army.

DE FOREST W. FERRIS, Co. E, March 11, 1862, commissioned 2d Lieut. Feb. 2, 1865, and mustered out August 21st of the same year.

EDWARD M. ABBOT, Co. A, March 16, 1864.

GEORGE BROWN, Co. B, Jan. 29, 1862.

*WILLIAM BROWN, Co. A, Oct. 15, 1863.

*HARRY BUSH, Co. D, Feb. 16, 1864.

JAMES B. CUNNINGHAM, Co, D, Dec. 31, 1863.

*CARL DIENER, Co. B, Oct. 20, 1863.

*CHARLES DREWER, Co. F, Oct 15, 1863.

ISAAC DINGER, Co. D, Feb. 20, 1864.

PATRICK FOX, Co. D, Nov. 7, 1862.

*EUGENE GAY, Co. H, Oct. 15, 1863.

STEPHEN GANUNG, Co. A, Feb. 25, 1864.

WILLIAM HALPIN, from Co. H, 28th Conn., Co. D, Sept. 5, 1864, mustered out June 26, 1865, at Goldsborough.

GEORGE HANFORD, Co. B, Feb. 29, 1862.

*JOSEPH HOOVEY, Co. F, Oct. 15, 1863.

JOHN HUNTER, Co F, Oct. 14, 1863.

JOHN J. HAIGHT, Co. D, Dec. 9, 1863.

John Hull, Co. A, Feb. 26, 1864.
Theron B. June, (?) Feb. 25, 1864.
*Henry Jackson, Co. C, Aug. 15, 1863.
Charles H. Krug, Co. E, Jan. 29, 1862.
*Frederick Kapp, Co. C, Oct. 12, 1863.
John Lawler, Co. B, Jan 29, 1862.
Chas. M. Lockwood, Co. K, Jan. 29, 1862.
*James Morann, Co. G, Oct. 10, 1863.
*James Morriss, Co. K, Oct. 15, 1863.
*Charles Newman, Co. H, Oct. 16, 1863.
William C. Oaks, Co. B, Feb. 19, 1862, discharged for disability Nov. 9, 1862; re-mus. Jan. 19, 1864.
David C. Palmer, Co. A, Feb. 19, 1862.   See Obituary.
John W. Pender, Co. B, Feb. 24, 1862.
George G. Smith, Co. B, Feb. 27, 1862.
Theophilus F. Smith, Co. B, Feb. 25, 1862.
Francis L. Still, Co. B, Feb. 11, 1862; transferred to signal corps U. S. Army.
Theodore C. Scofield, Co. K, March 1, 1862. See Obituary.
Clarence E. Searles, Co. D, Feb. 16, 1864; wounded in the arm at Deep Run.
*John Trechardt, Co. K, Oct 14, 1863.
Orlando Townsend, Co. D, Feb. 2, 1864.
Benj. S. Timson, Co. D, Feb. 20, 1864.
Nehemiah Taylor, Co. D, Feb. 23, 1864.
Samuel Waterbury, Co. D, Jan. 2, 1864.
John W. Daskam.   See Obituary.

Those with an asterisk (*) were substitutes or drafted men.

TENTH CONN.

COLONELS CHAS. L. RUSSEL, ALBERT W. DRAKE, IRA W.
PETTIBONE, JOHN L. OTIS, GEORGE W. WHITE
AND EDWIN S. GREELEY.

In Company G of this regiment, when it left Hartford, October 31, 1861, Stamford was represented by eighteen men, to whom were afterwards added from the town, in some of the companies of the regiment, seventeen new names. None of the Connecticut regiments won more distinction than the TENTH, and none of our Stamford companies did the town more credit than this. Leaving home under the captaincy of Isaac L. Hoyt,* and led by him, until seized by the disease which ended in his death, March 20, 1862, at Newbern, North Carolina—no company in any regiment could have been encouraged by the example of a a truer, or purer, or braver captain. Of its officers from Stamford, our obituary record must make additional report.

The regiment on receiving their colors, were forwarded to Annapolis, Md. On the evening of November 6, 1861, our men embarked with seven other companies on board the New Brunswick, under Burnside, in his memorable North Carolina expedition. To have endured uncomplainingly all the privations and discomforts of the voyage until they, at length, swung over the bar, into the Sound before Roanoke, was enough to commend to us the faithful men who were serving us. But let one of these townsmen, then "orderly," afterwards captain Greaves, show us what more than this uncomplaining endurance, what soldierly daring, also, these men had to commend them.

The letter from which we copy bears date Feb. 28, 1862, and this is its story:—" We finally left Hatteras, and after crawling carefully up the Sound for two or three days, we

---
*See Stamford History, page 307.

met the object of our visit—old Secesh, and gave him a salute. He was rather gruff and resentful of course, so we taught him a lesson or two in the art of throwing iron balls filled with a funny material which set fire to his wooden ware, and sent destruction to his domicile. He concluded to cut our acquaintance for a while, but the next morning he was around again. Then came the tug of war. February 8th was a day long to be remembered by those who took part in this conflict. We waded in mud and water to land, and fought in water and marsh till the cowards ran like sheep."

In another letter, he gives us this sketch of the struggle:— "At daylight the signal was given and we prepared for battle. In a few moments the battery took the lead, followed by the 23d and 27th Massachusetts, each with ambulance corps in the rear, and then came the Tenth Connecticut. The pickets maneuvered for some time in advance of us, but at eight o'clock the enemy's pickets had been driven in, and the famous three-gun masked battery opened upon the head of our column. We progressed very slowly and were soon met by the ambulance corps bringing back their boys that were killed or wounded. A few moments more and the Tenth Connecticut was drawn up, directly in front of the battery, about three hundred yards distance, while the Massachusetts boys worked themselves on either flank. Then came a dreadful volley of shot and shell, grape and canister, which was answered by our battery and muskets. The rebels gave it to us, in perfect hail storms, for a while, and our boys stood up with a bold front for two and a half hours, without a flinch."

Let us follow our boys a little further under the lead of the same graceful pen, and see how they managed another little affair for the good cause, in whose service they were now fairly embarked.

"After our boys had taken Elizabeth City, they saw a schooner in the distance and steamed for it. After coming along side, they hailed the schooner in the right nautical style, 'Whither bound?' 'Norfolk, with provisions,' was the captain's reply.

"'Please make fast,' promptly responded our officer in command, 'we'll take charge of your fixings.'

"The captain, with eyes fast opening to the situation, exclaimed, 'Who to thunder are you,' but at the same moment catching a glimpse of the Stars and Stripes, and expressed his peculiar astonishment by looks such as pen cannot describe.

"We found the schooner loaded with chickens, eggs, &c., which, of course, Commodore Goldsborough can appropriate to good advantage."

We will dwell a little longer with our Tenth boys, and hear our "orderly," who, at this date had become captain, report to us their part in the Kingston battle of Dec. 14, 1862.

"On the morning of the 14th, at eight o'clock, began the hardest fought battle that this Department has yet seen. It lasted some six hours, and closed by the Tenth Connecticut charging on the bridge and driving the men from their position. We suffered terribly, losing nearly a third of the men we took into action. I took only thirty-three men into action and lost nine. Lieut. Simms was badly wounded in the left shoulder, and is quite low. I was again among the uninjured. Though at the head of my company, and in front of them in the charge, I did not receive a scratch. It was a sorry day with the 'Old Tenth,' but she won golden honors of which she may be proud. After we had taken some 250 prisoners and had got possession of Kingston, Gen. Foster came past, and the boys gave him three hearty cheers.

He stopped his horse, and taking off his hat said: 'I never can pass the Tenth Connecticut without saying something. You have been with me through three hard fought battles, and to-day you have shown yourselves as you have always done, 'the bravest of the brave.'"

"From Kingston we went to Whitehall where we had another fight, which lasted some two hours. Our regiment was under fire most of the time. We then marched to the railroad bridge, six miles south of Goldsborough, where we had another battle, in which our artillery told fearfully on the ranks of the rebels. We drove them away and burned the bridge and spiles on which the road was built for some distance, and then returned to Newbern after an absence of ten days. We had marched 175 miles and fought three battles. We are now foot sore and weary, but expect in a few days to look after the enemy again, on another expedition of still greater magnitude."

But we must not dwell thus minutely on the several engagements in which this veteran regiment was engaged through the war. At the close of the period for which our Stamford men had enlisted, every man of them, who was still living, re-enlisted. And they were found, those of them who had strength enough left to follow in the army of the Union, as earnest in their devotion to the good cause in the last needed victory of Appomattox, July 9, 1865, as they had been in their earliest victories of Roanoke and Kingston.

A public presentation of a bronze eagle, on the 13th of June, 1865, was Maj-Gen. Gibbon's testimonial to the gallantry of the Tenth in the assault on Fort Gregg, July 2, 1865. It was not exaggerated praise which was given this regiment after three years' service: "It has ever held a foremost place in its brigade, its corps, and its department; and to-day no regiment in the entire army stands higher for gallantry, for discipline, for good morals, and for general efficiency."

The list of engagements in which the Tenth participated, as given in the Adjutant-General's report for 1866, are, Roanoke Island, Feb. 8, 1862; Newbern, N. C., March 14, 1862; Kingston, N. C., Dec. 14, 1862; Whitehall, N. C., Dec. 16, 1862; Seabrook Island, S. C., March 28, 1863; Siege of Charleston, S. C., from July 28 to Oct. 25, 1863; Near St. Augustine, Fla., Dec. 30, 1863; Walthall Junction, Va., May 7, 1864; Drury's Bluff, Va., May 13 to 17, 1864; Bermuda Hundred, Va., June 16, 1864; Strawberry Plains, Va., July 26 and 27, 1864; Deep Bottom, Va., Aug. 1st, and again Aug. 14, 1864; Deep Run, Va., Aug. 16, 1864; Siege of Petersburg, Va., Aug. 28 to Sept. 29, 1864; Laurel Hill Church, Va., Oct. 1, 1864; New Market Road, Va., Oct. 7, 1864; Darbytown Road, Va., Oct. 13 and 27, 1864; Johnson's Plantation, Va., Oct. 29, 1864; Hatcher's Run, Va., March 29 and 30, and April 1, 1865; Fort Gregg, Va., April 2, 1865, and Appomattox Court House, Va., April 9, 1865.

COMPANY G.

Mustered in October 2, 1861, re-enlisted veteran January 1, 1864, and mustered out August 25, 1865.

BENJAMIN L. GREAVES, chosen corporal on enlistment, Oct. 2, 1861, 1st sergeant, Jan. 1, 1862, and commissioned 2d Lieut. May 20th, 1st Lieut. Aug. 25th, and Capt. Oct. 25th of same year; mustered out on expiration of term of service, Oct. 25, 1864.   See Obituary.

THEODORE MILLER, commissioned 2d Lieut. Sept. 25, 1861, and resigned Dec. 4 of the same year. His name appears again with the 139th N. Y. State Militia.

JOHN M. SIMMS, mustered in Oct. 9, 1861, as 2d sergeant. Promoted 2d Lieut. Aug. 15, 1862.   See Obituary.

ANDREW F. JONES, re-enl. veteran, and com. 2d Lieut. Jan. 7, 1865, and wounded at Fort Gregg, a native of the town, now in New Canaan.

HENRY M. CAPPER, sergeant, Oct. 2, 1861. After a good record at the battle of Roanoke Island, Feb. 8, 1862, he was also in the engagement at Newbern of March 14, Having become lame he fell behind his company, when a solid shot shattered his right ankle, making amputation necessary. The leg was taken off above the knee, and at evening of the next day, he was taken to the hospital at Newbern. His cheerful courage here never failed him, and proved a God-send to many other wounded comrades. He was honorably discharged from the service, Sept. 21. 1862, and is now living in New Britain.

ALFRED C. ARNOLD, Aug. 28, 1862. He served twenty months in the Quarter Master's department at Fort Trumbull, Conn., and a year in conscript camp. He joined the regiment in Richmond in May, 1865, and was discharged June 15, 1865.

MORRIS CARROL, was wounded May 13, 1864. See Obituary.

SAMUEL B. HOYT, disch. for dis. Oct. 31, 1861. See Obituary.

ALFRED N. HUSTED, corporal, and re-enl. veteran.

THOMAS S. INGERSOLL, re-enl. veteran. See Obituary.

RUFUS S. KNAPP, re-enl. veteran.

SMITH O. KEELER, Oct. 9, 1861, from Ridgefield. On the skirmish line between Newbern and Kingston he was struck by a ball which, entering the palm of his hand, passed up the arm to the elbow. This being bent, the ball passed out, leaving the forearm so completely shattered, that amputation was necessary. He was honorably discharged Dec. 10, 1862, and with his family has been living here since 1863.

GEORGE E. LOCKWOOD, Oct. 16, 1861, discharged Oct. 28, 1861.

SIDNEY R. LOUNSBURY, re-enl. veteran, Feb. 19, 1864.

JAMES LYNOTT, re-enl. veteran.

EDMOND G. NUGENT, Oct. 9, 1861, and re-enl. vet. Feb. 6, 1864.

NICHOLAS N. NICHOLS was discharged for disability Feb. 22, 1863. Two others of his brothers, Joseph and John, both natives of the town, were in the service during the war, though not on the Stamford quota.

REUBEN PEATT, re-enl. veteran. See Obituary.
SAMUEL S. RAMBO, re-enl. veteran, Feb. 6, 1864.
SYLVANUS SMITH was discharged for disability, Dec. 18, 1861, and re-enl. into the 28th Conn. See Obituary.
HENRY TUCKER, Oct. 26, 1861, was a native of Stamford, and was discharged for disability, March 27, 1863. He re-enl. Dec. 24, 1863, and was wounded in the hip, Oct. 13, 1864.
ISAAC L. TUCKER, Oct. 26, 1861, also a native, re-enl. Dec. 24, 1863.
JOHN WHALEY was wounded at Deep Bottom, Aug. 14, 1864.

To the above we should add the following:

ALFRED BISHOP, who enlisted with the company and drilled with them in Hartford, until an attack of bleeding at the lungs disabled him. He afterwards applied to be mustered in and was rejected, but on being drafted still later, was passed by the surgeon. Finding himself unable to bear the exposure, he procured a substitute, entitling himself certainly to an honorary membership in the volunteer force.

RECRUITS.

JAMES M. CRAGUE, Co. C., Jan. 28, 1864.
BENJAMIN G. BLAKE, Co. D., Sept. 1, 1862.
JOHN B. NEWELL, Aug. 6, 1862, Co. D. Commissioned 2d Lieut. Jan. 7, 1865, and mustered out Aug. 25, 1865.
JAMES BARBER, Co. H., Dec. 26, 1863.
JOHN BOHAN, Co. I, Dec. 26, 1863.   See Obituary.
JOSEPH CORRIS, Co. I, Jan. 5, 1864.
WM. H. FERRIS, Co. I, Dec. 28, 1863.
WM. L. HAYS, Co. I, Jan. 25, 1863.
AARON J. MOGER, Co. I, Jan. 1, 1864.
AARON J. SHERWOOD, Co. I, Jan. 1, 1864.
JOHN SHERWOOD, Co. I, Jan. 1, 1865.

SEVENTEENTH CONN.

Colonel Wm. H. Noble.

In Company B of this regiment the town was represented by seventy-seven men when it left Camp Aiken, Bridgeport, September 3, 1862, for the seat of war. Before the war closed, in this, or in other companies of the regiment, nine other Stamford names were added to the list. Their first service was at Fort Marshall, Baltimore, Md., where they remained about a month, a part of the time sleeping on their arms, in expectation of an attack from Gen. Lee. After aiding in erecting defenses at Fort Kearney, they were ordered, November 3d, to report to Gen. Sigel, of the Eleventh Corps. Marching to Thoroughfare Gap, beyond Centreville, and finding no enemy, the regiment went into camp at Chantilly. They soon went into winter quarters at Brooks' Station. The reveille, of April 27, 1863, called our men again to the field, and, "fighting mit Sigel," there was no rest for them again until after the sharp work at Chancellorsville of May 2d, and our shattered and worn men had, without tents, without blankets, and on half rations, recrossed the Rappahannock "and crawled back wearily to Brooks' Station." Our roll will show that our men did not all return, and that of those who returned, not all were unscathed by the fiery touch of war.

Again, July 1st summoned our company to action. Meade has now the command, and he means to drive back the invaders from off Pennsylvania and across the last foot of Maryland soil. By the time the two armies had come well into striking distance, on the immortal field of Gettysburg, our townsmen in the Seventeenth are found occupying a perilous post on the front, in the right center, defending Cemetery Hill. Again and again the exultant rebels charge upon the position, and as often they were met by the steady and effective volleys which thinned and staggered their ranks, and which, at length, drove them back upon the town, broken and dispirited. No thunder of artillery, no screaming and crashing of shot or shell, no savage onset of Louisiana Tigers even, though thunder, and shot, and shell, and "Tigers" were hurled upon every sensibility they had, for those three mortal days, could chill the ardor of the daring men who there stood our representatives on that Thermopylæ of our strife. No company of Stamford men did severer or more daring work than this company found at Gettysburg. Our roll, at the end of this sketch, will report those of our men who fell, and those who were wounded or captured during these engagements.

As soon as they were permitted, our men are eagerly on the pursuit. By the 12th they reached Hagerstown, and captured one hundred and twenty-five prisoners. Early in August, the Seventeenth were ordered to Folly Island, and their gallant Colonel, now in charge of a brigade, is sent with a thousand men to the trenches before Fort Wagner.

February 23, 1864, they leave Folly Island for Jacksonville, Fla. April 25th they start on a foraging raid out to Volusia, seventy-five miles up the river from St. Augustine, and were successful. In May, Gen. Birney established pickets at Welaka and Saunders, eighty miles from St. Augustine, and left Captain Hobby and Lieut. Harvey, with portions of Company B, in command; and May 19th, thus exposed, they are surprised and captured by rebel cavalry. Our roll will also report these sons of the town in the personal sacrifices which they thus made for the cause.

The Adjutant-General of Connecticut, in his Report of 1866, names as the principal engagements in which this regiment participated, as: Chancellorsville, May 2, 1863; Gettysburg, July 1st–4th, 1863; Welaka and Saunders,

Fla., May 19, 1864; and Dunn's Lake, Fla., February 5, 1865.

After being mustered out at Hilton Head, the regiment left for home, reaching New Haven, August 3, 1865.

COMPANY B.

The men on this Roll were mustered in separately in 1862, and mustered out with the regiment, July 19, 1865.

ALLEN G. BRADY, Captain, Aug. 1, and promoted Major, Aug. 29, 1862. He had already done good service as Lieut.-Col. in the Third Conn., and approved himself as an energetic and daring officer. He was wounded at Gettysburg, and was discharged for disability, Oct. 21, 1863, having been appointed Major in the Invalid Corps.

MARCUS WATERBURY, commissioned Second Lieut. July 22, promoted First Lieut. July 21, 1862, and Capt. Co. I, Aug. 22, 1863. He was much on detailed duty during his service. At Chancellorsville, while repelling an attack on his flank, he was captured, with a number of his men, by a sudden movement from the front. After a month's imprisonment in Libby, he was exchanged. Both in his earlier and in his veteran service he won the name of a good soldier and most excellent officer.

CHARLES A. HOBBY, First Lieut., Aug. 1st, and promoted Capt. Aug 29, 1862. One of six brothers, the sons of Harvey Hobby, who were in the service, he made one of our best captains—considerate, careful, yet fearless and ready to share any danger to which he called his command. He was wounded May 2, 1863, at Brooks' Station, and taken prisoner, with his command, May 19, 1864, in Florida.

EDGAR HOYT, First Sergt., Aug. 6th, commissioned Second Lieut., Aug. 29, 1862, when his friends, of whom he had, as editor of our local paper, won many, presented him, through the Hon. M. F. Merritt, a splendid sword, sash and belt. Receiving an injury on the railroad between Washington and Baltimore, in the spring of 1863, he was compelled to resign May 12, 1863.

JOHN HARVEY, Sergt., July 25, 1862, commissioned First Lieut., Sept. 19, 1863, and promoted Capt., June 29, 1865.

GEO. A. SCOFIELD, Sergt., July 24, 1862. Was taken prisoner May 19, 1864, and released in the spring of 1865.

LEWIS W. SCOFIELD, Corp., July 28, 1864, was promoted sergeant, and taken prisoner at Welaka, May 19, 1864.

EDWIN O. HARRISON, Sergt., July 11, 1862. Taken prisoner May 2, 1863.

SELAH R. HOBBY, July 28, and promoted Sergt. He was wounded at Gettysburg, and taken prisoner in Florida, May 19, 1864.

MURRAY H. MACKEY, Corp., July 22, 1862, and promoted Sergt. See Obituary.

ALFRED V. SCOFIELD, Aug. 11, 1862, and chosen corporal. He was captured May 19, 1864.

EDWIN B. JESSUP, Corp., July 21, 1862. See Obituary.

CHRISTOPHER STOTTLAR, Corp., July 21, 1862. He was taken prisoner May 19, 1864.

EDSON C. BEARDSLEY, Corp., July 21, 1862.

MARTIN CASH, corporal, July 23, 1862; was taken prisoner in Florida, May 19, 1864, and sent to Andersonville. He was honorably discharged Nov. 25, 1864.

HENRY I. LOUNSBURY, musician, July 23, 1862. Discharged for disability, Feb. 7, 1863.

WILLIAM DUNHAM, musician, July 25, 1862, transferred to Invalid Corps, Sept. 1, 1863.

JOHN H. CHADWICK, Wagoner, July 18, 1862.

ELBERT AYRES, July 18, 1862; was taken prisoner at Chancellorsville and sent to Richmond, and again captured with his company in Florida.

DENNIS BURNS, Aug. 11, 1862, was discharged for disability Aug. 12, 1863.

JOHN BUTTRY, Aug. 9, 1862. See Obituary.

GEORGE B. CHRISTISON, Aug. 15, 1862, was wounded at Gettysburg.

EBENEZER S. CRABB, July 22, 1862, was transferred to Invalid corps, Feb. 15, 1864.

JOHN COLLINS, July 28, 1862; was wounded at Gettysburg.

GEORGE W. CHAMBERLAIN, July 18, 1862, transferred to U. S. cavalry.

MICHAEL EGAN, Aug. 12, 1862, was once reported as a deserter. A later report from one of the officers in his company amply vindicates his character. "There is not a more respectful, dutiful, obedient and brave soldier in the regiment."

GEORGE D. FEEKS, Aug. 11, 1862, was disch. for disability March 10, 1863, and re-enl. Jan. 28, 1864. See Obituary.

JOSEPH FEEKS, Aug. 6, 1862, was taken prisoner in Florida, May 19, 1864, and sent to Andersonville, Florence, Millen.

JOHN FITZPATRICK, Aug. 18, 1862, was transferred to veteran Reserve Corps Oct. 17, 1864, and honorably discharged July 13, 1865, at Elmira, N. Y.

PATRICK FITZPATRICK, Aug. 11, 1862; was transferred to the Pioneer Corps.

WILLIAM FARNOLD, Aug. 6, 1862.   See Obituary.

MICHAEL FOX, July 22, 1862.   See Obituary.

JOHN FARREL, July 19, 1862, prisoner at Chancellorsville.

WILLIAM GILLESPIE, July 31, 1862.   See Obituary.

THOMAS R. GRAHAM, Aug. 9, 1862.   See Obituary.

SAMUEL T. HALL, Aug. 2, 1862.

JOHN HARTMAN, July 29, 1862, re-enl., and once wounded.

GEORGE HEISER, Aug. 9, 1862, was taken prisoner at Chancellorsville and soon released.

MARTIN HEISER, July 15, 1862, a brother to GEORGE, was transferred to Veteran Reserve Corps, May 8, 1864, and taken prisoner in Florida, Feb. 5, 1865.

PATRICK HENNESY, July 18, 1862, was wounded at Chancellorsville.

ELI HOUNSLOW, July 26, 1862.

JOSEPH N. HOYT, Aug. 4, 1862.

LORENZO L. HOYT, July 25, 1862, taken prisoner May 19, 1864, and held six months. He was at length discharged from the hospital in Hartford, Aug. 5, 1865.

WM. H. JACKSON, July 25, 1862. He was singularly wounded at Gettysburg, in the midst of the fight, while lying down to load. The ball struck him between the shoulders, and passed under the skin, down the entire length of the spine. He was transferred to the Invalid Corps, Nov. 15, 1863, and left at the end of the war, with the record of a good soldier.

JOHN L. JUNE, Aug. 2, 1862, was wounded at Gettysburg, and taken prisoner in Florida, May 19, 1864.

JOHN KELLEY, 2d, July 28, 1862, was reported on the State catalogue as deserting, April 3, 1863.

DANIEL KENNEDY, Aug. 7, 1862, was discharged for disability, Jan. 16, 1863.

JACOB KREIG, Aug. 5, 1862.

GEORGE W. LINCOLN, July 29, 1862, was wounded at Chancellorsville, and transferred to Invalid Corps, July 1, 1863.

LEWIS MCDONALD, Aug. 11, 1862, was discharged for disability, Jan. 19, 1864.

GEO. H. MEEKER, joined this company in the spring of 1864, and was mustered out with the regiment.

CHARLES E. MORREL, Aug. 6, 1862.   See Obituary.

HUGH MAHAN, July 18, 1862.   See Obituary.

RICHARD MARLIN, Aug. 8, 1862, was discharged for disability, July 30, 1863.

LEWIS PARKETON, Aug. 1, 1862.

JOSEPH W. POTTS, Aug. 6, 1862.   See Obituary.

EDWARD H. QUIGLEY was taken prisoner at Welaka, Fla., and after a trial of rebel prison life in Andersonville, Millen and Florence, was exchanged, Feb. 27th, and discharged at Fort Schuyler, June 10, 1865.

JOHN RITKE, Aug. 11, 1862, was discharged for disability, May 21, 1863.

JACOB STOTILAR, July 18, 1862, was transferred to Invalid Corps, Sept. 30, 1863.
WILLIAM T. STEVENS, July 21, 1862.   See Obituary.
ALBERT STEVENS, July 29, 1862.   See Obituary.
JAMES THEODORE SCOFIELD, July 24, 1862.
SAMUEL SCOFIELD, July 25, 1862, was discharged by court-martial, Dec. 19, 1863.
WILLIAM H. SCOFIELD, Aug. 7, 1862, was discharged for disability, Feb. 9, 1863.
EDWIN L. SMITH, July 26, 1862, was transferred to Invalid Corps, July 1, 1863, and to Co. A, Ninth U. S. Reserves.
MORTIMER SEARLES, Aug. 6, 1862, was wounded at Gettysburg, and taken prisoner in Florida, May 19, 1864.
GEORGE STEINERT, Aug. 7, 1862, was discharged for disability, March 28, 1863.
JOHN SMALART, Aug. 7, 1862, is reported as deserting at Baltimore, Sept. 28, 1862.
JACOB VANDERHOFF was taken down with typhoid fever before the regiment went to the front. He joined the regiment in St. Augustine, Fla., in the spring of 1864.
EMANUEL VANDERVALDT, July 28, 1862, and reported deserting, Sept. 4, 1862.
JACOB W. VINCENT, Aug. 5, 1862.   See Obituary.
JOSEPH VOID, July 22, 1862, wounded May 2, 1863, and taken prisoner in Florida, May 19, 1864.
JOHN WESLEY WALTERS, Aug. 8, 1862, was taken prisoner at Chancellorsville, May 2, 1863, and returned to the regiment Oct. 12, 1863. He was honorably discharged July 17, 1865.
GEORGE WEED, Aug. 2, 1862, was captured in Florida, May 19, 1864.
EDWARD WHALEY, Aug. 13, 1862, taken prisoner in Florida, May 19, 1864.
JOHN H. WILSON, Aug. 6, 1862, and discharged for disability, Feb. 9, 1863.
WILLIAM WILLIAMS, July 28, 1862, was reported as deserter, Sept. 4, 1862.

MILITARY SERVICE.—TWENTY-EIGHTH CONN.   73

JOHN D. BUTTRY, Co. A, Aug. 4, 1862, wounded in the leg, July 2, 1863, at Gettysburg, taken prisoner and sent to Belle Isle; paroled June 28th, 1864, and went to Haddington Hospital, Philadelphia, where he was honorably discharged, Aug. 27, 1864.

SAMUEL C. MORRISON, Co. A, Aug. 8, 1862, from Norwalk.

JOHN W. STOCKTON, Co. E, March 5, 1864.

GEORGE HOYT, Co. F, Aug. 22, 1862, from Norwalk, was taken prisoner at Chancellorsville, and held two weeks by the rebels.

LEVI DIXON, Co. H, Aug. 20, 1862, had his right leg shattered at Gettysburg, July 1, 1863. A rebel surgeon amputated his leg on the 2d, and on the 4th he was recaptured by our men and taken into hospital. He was honorably discharged, Oct. 4, 1864, and is pensioned. He enlisted from New Canaan, but is a citizen of Stamford.

SAMUEL S. OSBORN, Co. H, Aug. 12, 1862, and discharged for disability, April 30, 1863. He re-enlisted into Co. M, Second Conn. Art.

LEVI ST. J. WEED, Corp., Co. H, Aug. 18, 1862.

DAVID C. COMSTOCK, JR., Co. H, Aug. 12, 1862, was disch. for disability, to enlist as Hospital Steward, U. S. A.

ALFRED Z. BRODHURST, Co. H, July 29, 1862.

GEORGE W. WEED, Co. H, Aug. 22, 1862, from the Seventy-first N. Y. Infantry.

WARREN KIRK, Corp., Co. K, Aug. 15, 1862, was transferred to Veteran Reserve Corps, March 15, 1864.

TWENTY-EIGHTH CONN.
COL. SAMUEL P. FERRIS.

Mustered in November 15, 1862, and discharged August 28, 1863.

In this nine months' regiment, which consisted of eight companies, Stamford was more fully represented than in any other regiment of the State. The colonel of the regiment, a son of the Hon. J. B. Ferris, of Stamford, had received his military education at West Point, and graduated as 2d Lieut. on the opening of the war, directly into the practice of his profession. He had declined a lieutenant-colonel's commission in the Seventeenth Conn., and received one of colonel in the Twenty-Eighth, on its organization. Before the return of the regiment, five of the colonel's staff also were Stamford men. Composed so largely of our citizens, both in the ranks and on the field and staff, this regiment could but excite the deepest interest of our citizens. Of this interest our opening chapter has already spoken.

For my account of the movements of this regiment, I am largely indebted to the printed or manuscript record, made by the careful pen of captain Charles H. Brown, now of Washington city.

The regiment was organized October 11, 1862, at Camp Aiken, New Haven. After receiving their clothing and equipments they were mustered into the United States service, Nov. 15th, and on the 18th they went on board the Elm City, and proceeded to camp Buckingham, L. I. They were assigned to the Department of the South, under Gen. Banks, and on Saturday the 28th, they again struck tents in a severe rain storm, and embarked on the Che Kiang for their Southern destination. With them also embarked the Twenty-third Conn., thus crowding on board a steamer which might have given comfortable quarters to some 800 troops about 1,400 Connecticut soldiers.

The steamer weighed anchor at ten o'clock, December 3d, under first orders to sail south twenty-four hours, and then open the orders which should direct the subsequent course of the expedition. The second orders, when opened, assigned Ship Island, La., as the immediate destination of the steamer.

On Friday the 5th, at noon, as if to test the quality of our men, a sudden gale and storm arose. By night the ocean tempest seemed to be doing its best. The steamer, heavily loaded, hatches down, and everything on board prepared for a fearful strife, rolled, and pitched, and groaned. "The storm," wrote Captain Brown, "was grand and terrible, far beyond description. Those on board will never forget it, nor forget the prayers which were then uttered for safety."

During the progress of the conflict, one of the officers who had been fast by the life-boat for hours, in answer to the inquiry, "What is the prospect?" answered, "We shall never see another sunrise, the vessel cannot stand it much longer."

But the morning came, greatly to the comfort, as well as safety, of our imperiled and imprisoned men; and not a man of them can be found who would wish another such encounter with an angry ocean storm. The rest of the voyage was delightful, as if to make amends for the discomfort and fear of that stormy night. Nothing exciting occurred on the passage, excepting that while off the Tortugas, a small sail vessel ran into the Che Kiang, striking her just forward of the wheel-house, and damaging her to the tune of some six thousand dollars. As the suspected craft fell astern of the steamer, our band on board struck up in liveliest time our "Yankee Doodle." It was afterwards learned that the assailing craft was only a pilot boat, and that the collision was accidental.

On Friday morning December 12th, our men landed on Ship Island, until the steamer could be repaired. After landing and pitching their tents our men enjoyed a night's repose on land, though their beds were of the soft sands, which a southern wind storm might at any time set to rolling about as the billowy ocean they had just escaped.

While here, our boys making the best of the situation, extracted such fun and comfort as their condition and means could supply, little caring what the sober, outside world, civil or military, might think of their pranks. Who will complain if some dexterous right hand among them, baiting his hook skillfully, should deftly draw the plumpest fowl out of a neighboring henery, and in as few minutes as it takes to tell the story, have it roasting scientifically for the longing palates it was destined to satisfy?

On Wednesday, the 17th, the two regiments re-embarked for New Orleans, and, after stopping a few hours in the city, started for Camp Parapet, some seven miles up the river, where they landed and pitched tents; but were immediately ordered to re-embark for Pensacola, Fla. By eleven that night they were on board again, and ready for starting. They reached Pensacola Monday morning, and stacked their arms in the "Grand Plaza." On the 20th, they were ordered to evacuate Pensacola and go to the Barrancas Navy Yard, where they remained until May 10th, when they were ordered to take the steamer Crescent and proceed to Brashear City, La. On the 25th, they were ordered to Port Hudson, and at noon reached Springfield Landing, having now come within hearing distance of the strife of arms. Marching twelve miles toward the scene of conflict, they found themselves now, by some oversight of the movement, right between the two contending armies. They fairly ran the gauntlet, escaping unharmed, and, the next day, after a march of about thirty miles, when four might have sufficed, they reached Grover's Division, to which they had been assigned. Until June 3d they here suffered, as soldiers often do, for want of rest and food, when they were ordered to the front.

Colonel Ferris, as Acting Brigadier, and major Wescome, in charge of the regiment. Capt. Jones, of Co. B, was appointed Aid to the colonel, Lieut. Warner, Assistant-

Adjutant-General, and Lieut. Bennet Acting Adjutant of Brigade. Our men were now called to test the music of whistling balls, and there was, for the present, to be no more rest for them. June 4th they are ordered to be ready to go into the rifle-pits. In spite of blundering movements, Co. A in advance, they at length reach the pits, where they spent the night. The next day, until eight in the evening, our men did their best, "firing fast and well," to harm the enemy, when they were ordered back to camp. This move was executed without loss, and the regiment next did good service in the trenches.

On Friday, the 12th, orders came for a detail of one hundred men, for a storming party. From Stamford, on that detail, were Capt. Brown, of Co. A, in command of the detail from Cos. A, C, G and H, with Sergt. Stiles Raymond, and privates I. Barret, S. S. Dixon, Smith Scofield, A. S. Selleck, J. Wardell, J. Lower, H. Mead, H. Jimmerson, J. V. Swertcope, F. Hayward, and C. A. Rosborough.

To the credit of Sergeant Stiles Raymond, it should be put on record that he was not regularly detailed for this hazardous service. George A. Mead his fellow-sergeant had been detailed, and as he had left behind him a wife and little one to await his return, his comrade, Stiles Raymond, a single man, volunteered to take his place on the forlorn hope.

It should also be reported here, to the credit of a citizen of the town, Wm. W. Saunders, that he volunteered to take the place of a detailed man of the regiment, and that he barely escaped from the death storm of that fearful charge, having had the hammer of his musket struck off by a shot which otherwise might have found his heart.

Nor must we omit from this roll of credit the special

service of Joseph Paight. When the hour for assault had come, the color-bearer of the regiment had failed. The Colonel called for a volunteer. There was some hesitation at assuming a post of so eminent risk, but not long. Joseph Paight stepped forward and accepted the risk, carrying thenceforward the regimental flag, which, in his trusty hands, was never disgraced.

It was no ordinary service, even in war, which these men, thus detailed, were called to do; and they saw, as we now cannot see, the fearful risks before them. Thoughtfully they prepared themselves for the duty. They wrote, many of them the last messages of love to the dear ones at home which they ever expected to pen. They made careful preparation for the charge. The next morning (Saturday) they were formed in line, and notified that the charge was to be made at two o'clock the next morning, Sunday. At three p. m. they were again formed and marched out on the Jackson road, where they stacked their arms for rest. At midnight they were called up. Hand grenades were given them—though no one of the detail had probably ever before attempted to use them, and of which there was no time now to secure the skillful use. At two o'clock the order to march finds every man at his post. Reaching the field in front of the batteries, they meet a furious storm of shot and shell, and escape the hurtling death by falling down between the corn hills. At four, the order is given to advance. With a cheer they start, but their line, broken up by a heavy hawthorn hedge, through whose only opening they had to go, they could not again re-form. Reaching the ditch they were checked, and at that distance the hand grenades were found of little use, and the assault proved ineffectual. The slaughter of our men in the assault was fearful. From Stamford, Lieut. Durand fell while beckoning his men to the charge. Corporal Vail and private Wardell quickly followed him. C. A. Rosborough met the wounds which, ere another month, was to take him to their company again. And our catalogue of these companies will show who besides were to bear in their bodies the tokens of their valor and their peril in this assault.

One only of our whole number, the wiry and active Geo. A. Waterbury, succeeded in crossing over the enemy's breastworks, and he was, of course, a prisoner in their hands.

At dusk the order is given to retire, and of those from Co. A, who left the field together, were captain Brown and privates Lower, Swertcope and Barret.

During the day of the charge, our men, both of the assaulting party and of the rest of the regiment, had to save themselves by lying down as the shots of the enemy passed over them. In their desperation, hot, hungry and thirsty, as they were, some of the more resolute of them attempted to cross the field which was most completely raked by their fire. Lieut. Daskam, while running the gauntlet, had his cap carried off by a rebel shot. It was only after the night had set in that our forces could return to their position before the charge. Yet, after the return, worn and shattered as they were, a detail of twenty-four men was ordered to support a battery, and Sergeant Mead, of Company A, was still ready for the command.

On the 16th it was found that Company A had seventeen men, and B only five fit for duty. By the next day, however, they were mainly ready for duty, and nobly reported themselves in the rifle-pits to which they were ordered. Gen. Banks sent in a flag of truce that we might recover and bury our dead, and the bodies of our three men who had fallen were brought off from the field and buried near the picket fence.

On the 20th, the regiment was ordered to report to Gen. Weitzel, to go to Jackson. They executed the order, Lieut. Lever in command of Company A, Lieut. Wilmot, of Company B, and Lieut. Daskam acting adjutant; and they returned on the 23d. June 26th, companies A and B, commanded as above, were ordered into the trenches on fatigue duty. July 5th, Capt. Brown took command of the rifle pits. After the surrender of Port Hudson, July 8th, our regiment was ordered to picket duty in the vicinity, and Capt. Brown was detailed to parole prisoners.

Thus far no unsoldierly conduct was chargeable upon either of the companies which represented us, unless that of Company B, on the 4th of June, for allowing its lines to be broken, and for which the colors of the regiment had been taken away and transferred to Company C. On the 15th of July a court of inquiry sat upon the case, and Capt. Jones was acquitted of all blame in the matter.

On the 18th, when the regiment was inspected, Company A reported 34 and Company B, 22 men for duty. Since May 20th, the regiment, having left their tents at Baton Rouge, had slept on the ground. Their baggage reached them July 23d, and August 3d, orders for the regiment to go inside of fortifications. August 7th, at half-past ten, A. M., the long delayed and wished for orders were received for the regiment to start for home. Leaving their arms at the ordnance office, at 5 A. M., our men went on board the steamer Madison, and at half-past nine steamed away, up the river, from Port Hudson, and the Department of the Gulf.

And now the service of our men begins to tell upon those men who have survived the carnage of the battle-field. One and another, and still others drop off as the steamer plows its way up the stream, and sorrowful hands lay them to their last rest on its banks. Others of the worn ones are obliged to stop on the passage, wherever a friendly hospital offers them a chance to prolong the lives which continued journeying will certainly and quickly end.

Reaching Cairo on the 15th, they leave the next evening by railroad for the East. The returning men found their journey homeward an ovation worthy of heroes. At Indianapolis, Cleveland, Buffalo, Utica and Albany, whether the arrival was at noontide or midnight, our soldiers found sumptuous preparations for their entertainments; and all along the way, at the smallest towns, and from the doors of hamlets on the roadside, the welcome they received was the award of a grateful and loyal people.

FIELD AND STAFF.

SAMUEL PETERS FERRIS, Oct. 18, 1862, and honorably discharged August 28, 1863. His record on the field was that of an admirable tactician, handling his regiment or brigade with great dexterity and skill. His record again appears on the roll of the United States Army.

CHARLES H. BROWN, Adjutant, October 18, 1862, promoted captain Company A, February 20, 1863.

FREDERICK R. WARNER, Adjutant, February 20, 1863, and honorably discharged August 28, 1863; and enlisted into the Hawkins' Zouaves.

WILLIAM A. BAILEY, Sergeant-major, October 18, 1862, honorably discharged August 28, 1863.

NELSON B. BENNET, commissary sergeant, September 10, 1862, honorably discharged August 28, 1863.

HENRY ROCKWELL, M. D., 2d assistant surgeon, November 26, 1862, honorably discharged August 28, 1863, and appointed surgeon in the U. S. Army.

COMPANY A.

FRANCIS R. LEEDS, enlisted August 12th, and commissioned September 1, 1862. See Obituary.

CHARLES H. BROWN, August 12, 1862, 1st Lieut. September

1st, appointed adjutant October 18, 1862, and promoted captain February 20, 1863. Our record of the assault on Port Hudson, is ample testimony to his merit as soldier and officer. His name is deservedly high on our Stamford roll.

PHILIP LEVER, August 12, 1862, 2d Lieut. September 1st, and 1st Lieut. October 24, 1862. He was a spirited and efficient officer.

FREDERICK R. WARNER, August 25, 1862, 2d Lieut. October 24th, and adjutant February 20, 1863. He had already seen service in the Ninth New York, and been wounded at Harper's Ferry, July 4, 1861. He was energetic in action and severe in discipline. After his discharge with the regiment he re-enl. into the 64th N. Y.

EUGENE B. DASKAM, 1st sergeant August 16, 1862, and 2d Lieut February 20, 1863. A popular officer, now in the service of the Treasury Department, Washington, D. C.

ASHBEL W. SCOFIELD, sergeant. Aug. 25, 1862, left in hospital at Cleveland, Aug. 18, 1863.

STILES RAYMOND, sergeant, Aug. 14, 1862. See page 77.

STEPHEN S. SMITH, sergeant, Aug. 29, 1862.

GEORGE A. MEAD, sergeant, Aug. 20 1862. See page 77, also Obituary.

SEYMOUR J. BODEY, corporal, Aug. 13, 1862, and appointed quartermaster's-sergeant.

ROBERT BUNTEN, corporal, Aug. 12, 1862.

ALEXANDER WEED, corporal Aug. 12, 1862.

ALONZO S. MORGAN, color corporal, Aug. 14, 1862, left sick at Cleveland Aug. 18, 1863.

WM. O. WEBB, corporal, Aug. 12, 1862.
                                                    See Obituary.
GABRIEL W. PLATT, corporal, Aug. 20, 1862.
                                                    See Obituary.
JAMES VAIL, corporal, Aug. 30, 1862.   See Obituary.

WELLS R. WHITNEY, Aug 12, and appointed Ordnance Sergt.

JACOB WATERS, musician, Aug. 81, 1862, discharged.

HENRY J. HOWELL, musician, Sept. 10, 1862.
PHILIP B. KEELER, wagoner, Aug. 18, 1862.
CHARLES J. BROWN, Aug. 19, 1862, left in Cleveland sick, August 1, 1863.
SEELY BROWN, Aug. 27, 1862.
ISAAC BARRETT, Aug. 19, 1862, wounded in the foot, June 14, 1862.
AARON BILLINGS, Aug. 21, 1862; left sick in Memphis Aug. 13, 1862.
ISAAC BILLINGS, Aug. 25, 1862.
ADAM F. BILLINGS, Aug. 25, 1862.
JOHN E. BOUTON, Aug. 25, 1862.   See Obituary.
THEODORE W. BOUTON, Aug. 27, 1862.
WM. C. BOUTON, Sept. 10, 1862, deserted, arrested and discharged Dec. 6, 1863.
WM. H. BOUTON, Aug. 28, 1862, honorably discharged.
SPENCER BOUTON, Aug. 30, 1862.   See Obituary.
JAMES N. BUXTON, Aug 28, 1862, deserted Nov. 29, 1862.
JAMES B. CUNNINGHAM, Aug. 22, 1862, honorably discharged and re-enlisted in Sixth Conn.
GEORGE CRABB, Aug. 25, 1862.
GEORGE R. CRABB, Sept. 10, 1862.
GEORGE W. CLOCK, Aug. 27, 1862.   See Obituary.
SMITH DANN, Aug. 23, 1862.
STEPHEN S. DIXON, Aug. 25, 1862.
JAMES N. FERRIS, Aug. 18, 1862, discharged Dec. 3, 1863.
EDWARD A. FERRIS, Oct. 30, 1862.
ALBERT E. FARRINGTON, Aug. 26, 1862.
JOEL M. GILBERT, Aug. 25, 1862.
ALEX. J. HOLLY, Aug. 13, 1862.
JOHN E. HOYT, Aug. 13, 1862.   See Obituary.
NOAH W. HOYT, Aug. 23, 1862.
FREDERICK HAYWARD, Aug. 26, was wounded in the storming party, June 14th.

Harrison Hicks, Aug. 27, 1862.
John D. Jessup, Aug. 28, 1862.
Henry F. Jimmerson, Sept. 1, 1862.
Theodore Knapp, Aug. 25th, left in hospital, Memphis, Aug. 13, 1863.
Chas. W. Litchfield, Aug. 20, 1862,   See Obituary.
John Lower, Sept. 1, left sick at Cleveland Aug. 18, 1863.
Henry Lower, Aug. 23, 1862.   See Obituary.
Andrew J. Lockwood, Aug. 27, 1862.   See Obituary.
Sherman D. Lockwood, Aug. 26, 1862.   See Obituary.
Thos. W. Mollet, Aug. 13, 1862.   See Obituary.
Hanford Mead, Aug. 25, 1862.
Lewis Provost, Aug. 26, 1862. Sick in hospital, at Brashear City when the company left.
Alonzo L. Parker, Aug. 30, 1862.
Theodore H. Peck, Aug 30, 1862.   See Obituary.
Cyrus J. Raymond, Aug. 15, 1862.
Jerome Rafferty, Aug 15, 1862.
Chas. A. Rosborough, Aug. 26, 1862.   See Obituary.
Stephen Smith, Aug. 12, 1862.
George R. Searles, Aug. 20, 1862.   See Obituary.
Geo E. Scofield, Aug. 14, 1862.
Sylvester L. Scofield, Aug. 25, 1862.
Smith Scofield, Aug. 26, 1862.
Loomis Scofield, Aug. 26, 1862.
Gilbert Scofield, Aug. 20, 1862.   See Obituary.
John V. Sweetcope, Aug. 18, 1862.
Henry A. Sherwood, Aug 23, 1862.
Nathan Sherwood, Aug. 27, 1862.   See Obituary.
Arba S. Selleck, Aug. 25, 1862.
Wm. H. Totten, Aug. 25, 1862.   See Obituary.
Wm. S. Taylor, Aug. 27, in hospital at Brashear City when the company left.
Geo. W. Todd, Aug. 30, 1862.

MILITARY SERVICE.—CO. B, TWENTY-EIGHTH CONN.   85

Henry M. Whitney, Aug. 18, left sick at Cleveland, Aug. 18, 1863.
Edmund M. Williams, Aug. 13, 1863.
Jason Wardell, Aug. 18, 1863.   See Obituary.
Andrew C. Waterbury, Aug. 26, 1862.   See Obituary.
Stephen R. Waterbury, Aug. 26, 1862. See Obituary.
Ammi L. Wessels, Aug. 27, 1862.

COMPANY B.

Cyrus D. Jones, Aug. 29, and com. Capt. Sept. 30, 1863.
Charles Durand, Sept. 3d, 1st Lieut. Sept. 13, 1862. See Obituary.
Henry L. Wilmot, Aug. 30, 2d Lieut. Sept. 13, 1862.
Abel Tanner, 1st sergeant Sept. 8, 1862.
Benjamin W. Card, Serg. Sept. 10, 2d Lieut. July 23, 1863, on detailed service.
Andrew Boyd, Sergt. Sept. 8, 1862.   See Obituary.
Geo. A. Waterbury, Sergt. Aug. 30, taken prisoner July 14th, at Port Hudson, and released July 14th.
Charles H. Conley, Sergt., Sept. 10, 1862.
Lewis Jones, Corp., Sept. 9, 1862.
Charles Weed, Corp., Sept. 10, 1862.
Edmund P. Bailey, Corp., Sept. 30, 1862.
Wm. H. King, Corp., Sept. 10, 1862.
James H. Nichols, Corp., Sept. 2, 1862.
David C. Scofield, Sept. 10, 1862.
Eben. R. Lawrence, Corp., Sept. 10, 1862.
Geo. A. Eldridge, musician, Aug. 30, 1862.
Samuel M. Bouton, musician, Aug. 30, 1862.
Chas. L. Weed, wagoner, Sept. 8, 1862.
Elah Ballard, Aug. 30, 1862.
Wm. H. Banks, Sept. 3, 1862.
Nath'l. Barmore, Jr., Sept. 9, 1862.   See Obituary.
Charles Bell, Sept. 10, 1862.

NELSON BENNETT, Corp. Sept. 13, 1862, and soon, commissary sergeant, returning to his Co. Jan. 13, 1863.
GEO. R. BUNTEN, Sept. 11, 1862. Sick in Utica, when the regiment was mustered out.
JOHN BUTCHER, Sept. 13, 1862, reported a deserter, Nov. 18, 1862.
CHAS. W. CALDWELL, Sept. 8, 1862.
SAMUEL CALDWELL, Sept. 13, 1862. See Obituary.
EDWARD T. CLARK, Sept. 4, 1862. See Obituary.
WM. H. CRABB, Sept. 6, 1862. In hospital, at Memphis, Aug. 13, 1862.
ANDREW CRISSY, Oct. 3, 1862. In hospital, at Brashear City, May 23, 1862.
ORIGEN S. ENSLEY. Left sick at New Haven, Nov. 8, 1862.
AARON P. FERRIS, Sept. 10, 1862, disch. disability, July 27, 1863, at Port Hudson, La.
BENJ. P. FERRIS, Sept. 3, 1862.
ISAAC FERRIS, Sept. 2, 1862.
JOEL G. FOSTER, Aug. 30, 1862, appointed corporal Oct. 18.
PETER FRYERMUTH, Sept. 11, 1862, disch. for disability, Jan. 19, 1863.
JOHN GAGAN, Sept. 15, 1862.
ISAAC F. HOYT, Sept. 2, 1862.
SETH H. HOYT, Sept. 10, 1862. See Obituary.
ANDREW HOYT, Sept. 10, 1862. See Obituary.
LYMAN HOYT, Sept. 10, 1862.
HIRAM S. HOLLY, Sept. 6, 1862.
WM. L. HALL, Sept. 10, 1862.
GEO. W. HARISON, Sept. 4, 1862. See Obituary.
NAHOR JONES, Sept. 10, 1862.
ALVA JONES, Sept. 11, 1862, wounded, June 14th, at Port Hudson.
HENRY R. JACKSON, Sept. 10, 1862.
WM. H. JUNE, Sept. 11, 1862, was in the assault on Port Hudson, June 14th.

MILITARY SERVICE.—CO. B, TWENTY-EIGHTH CONN.

GEO. W. JUNE, Sept. 11, 1862, was in the assault on Port Hudson, June 14th.
CHARLES JENNINGS, Sept. 11, 1862. See Obituary.
CHARLES W. KNAPP, Jr., Sept. 10, 1862.
FREDERICK LOWE, Sept. 4, 1862, reported deserter, Nov. 14, 1862.
SAMUEL LOCKWOOD, 2nd, Sept. 10, 1862.
SAMUEL R. LOCKWOOD, Sept. 10, 1862.
WM. H. LOCKWOOD, Sept. 24, 1862.
THOMAS LOWNEY, Sept. 11, 1862, reported deserter, Nov. 18, 1862.
CHARLES W. MILLER, Sept. 2, 1862. See Obituary.
THOMAS NODYNE, Sept. 6, 1862.
ELIAS E. PALMER, Sept. 13, 1862, wounded at Port Hudson, June 14th.
HENRY H. ROSCOE, Sept 9, 1862.
DANIEL RANDALL, Sept. 11, 1862.
CHARLES J. RUSHER, Nov. 18, 1862, wounded July 6, before Port Hudson, while crossing an exposed opening before the rifle pits.
SYLVANUS SMITH, Sept. 3, 1863. See Obituary.
CHARLES L. SMITH, Sept. 10, 1862, wounded at Port Hudson, June 14, 1863.
SELLECK S. SCOFIELD, Sept. 6, 1862.
GEORGE E. SCOFIELD, Sept 10, 1862, and appointed commissary sergeant.
LEWIS B. SCOFIELD, Sept. 10, 1862. See Obituary.
WM. SCOFIELD, Sept. 11, 1862.
JAMES E. SCOFIELD, Sept. 11, 1862; in hospital at Brashear City, May 23, 1863.
NOAH FRANKLIN SCOFIELD, Sept 13, 1862.
WM. W. SAUNDERS, Sept. 10, 1861. See page 77.
GEO. E. SAUNDERS Sept. 11, 1862.
JOHN SLATER, Sept. 13, 1862, reported deserter Nov. 18, 1862
THOMAS STANLEY, Sept. 23, 1862.

WM. H. STEVENS. Oct. 3, 1862, reported deserter Nov. 1862.
SAMUEL A. WOOD, Sept 3, 1862, wounded June 14, 1863, at Port Hudson.
CHARLES W. WATERBURY, Sept. 3, 1862.
PHILIP WATERBURY, Sept. 10, 1862.
JOSEPH WILMOT, Sept. 8, 1862, reported deserter Nov. 18, 1862.
JAMES T. WILMOT, Sept. 10, 1862.
WILLIAM H. WALTON, Sept. 10, 1862.   See Obituary.
WILLIAM H. WARING, Sept. 23, 1862.
THADDEUS L. BAILEY, May 12, 1862.   See Obituary.
JOSEPH PAIGHT, Sergt., Sep.. 9, 1862.   See page 78.
FRANCIS H. JONES, Aug. 27, 1862, and was in the storming party July 14th, at Port Hudson. He re-enlisted July 23, 1863.
CLEMENT E. MILLER, Aug. 25, 1862.
NATHANIEL H. NICHOLS, Oct. 7, 1862
MILES J. STEPHENS, Aug. 22, 1862.
ADDISON P. SCOFIELD, Aug. 20, 1862.
JOHN WATERS, Aug. 25, 1862.   See Obituary.
GEORGE W. WILMOT, Aug. 9, 1862.   See Obituary.
GEO. H. MEEKER, Corp. Co. G, Sept. 8, 1862, and re-enl. into 17th Conn. Vol., having enlisted from Norwalk but now living here.

COMPANY H.

RICHARD ARMSTRONG, Aug. 19, 1862. After discharge re-enl., and has never been heard from, leaving here a wife and one child.
PHINEAS BROWN, Aug. 22, 1862.
THEODORE DELCROIX, Aug. 15, 1862.
CORNELIUS DEVER, Aug. 20, 1862.
WRIGHT H. FEEKS, Aug. 20, 1862, and was later in a New York regiment.
WILLIAM HALPIN, Aug. 13, 1862, re enl. 6th Conn.

THOMAS LAWLER, Aug. 25, 1862, storming party, June 14th, wounded in shoulder.
HIBBARD MEAD, Aug. 28, 1862.   See Obituary.
THOMAS O'BRIEN, Jr., Aug. 18, 1862.   See Obituary.
JOSEPH A. SUTTON, Aug. 18, 1862.   See Obituary.

OTHER CONNECTICUT REGIMENTS.
FIRST.
WILLIAM KELLER, Rifle Co. B, April 22, 1861, and disch. for disability April 24, 1861.
ALLEN WEBB, Co. H, April 23, 1861, honorably discharged July 31, 1861, and re-enl. into the 2d Conn. Light Battery.

SECOND.
JOHN LILLEY, Co. B, May 7, 1861, from Norwich. He was honorably discharged as first sergeant Aug. 7, 1861, and re-enl. into the 17th Conn.

FOURTH.
JOHN A. HOLTON, M. D., Co. I, afterwards 1st Artillery, June 12, 1861, and discharged March 29, 1862. He was here as a dentist on the opening of the war. It is believed he was commissioned assistant surgeon and assigned to hospital duty.

FIFTH.
WILLIAM H. CARD, Co. A, July 22, 1861, discharged for disability Jan. 29, 1862.
THOMAS M. WELSH, Co. A, July 22, 1861.
MICHAEL COLLINS, Co. K, April 6, 1864.

SEVENTH.
GROSVENOR STARR, Adjutant, Sept. 17, 1861.   See Obituary.
GEORGE ADAMS, Co. A, Sept. 5, 1861, re-enl. Dec. 22, 1863, and reported a deserter.
JOHN H. VERNAL, musician, Co. I, Sept. 13, 1861.
LEWIS A. COOK, Co. E, Sept. 7, 1861, and re-enl. vet. See Obit.

EIGHTH.
JAMES CONLAN, Oct. 5, 1861, re-enl. veteran, Dec. 24, 1863.

TIMOTHY CAHILL, Sept. 23, 1861, from Norwalk. He was honorably discharged at Bermuda Hundred, and is now living here.

NINTH.

JAMES COLLINS, Feb. 17, 1863, to June 30, 1864.
JOHN CONNELLY, April 25, 1864, to June 30, 1864.
THOMAS IRVING, April 30, 1864, to June 30, 1864.

ELEVENTH.

HENRY BERESFORD, April 11, 1864, to June 30, 1864.
WILLIAM CHANEY, April 19, 1864, to June 30, 1864.
JAMES FARREL, April 23, 1864, to June 30, 1864.
WILLIAM JOHNSON, Feb. 27, 1864, to June 30, 1864.
FRANK McQUEON, Co. D, May 3, 1864.
PIERRE POINSETT, Co. C, May 10, 1864.
PETER SIMPSON, Co. G, April 23, 1864.

TWELFTH.

EBENEZER NORMAN, Co. E, Nov 19, 1861. Discharged for disability July 17, 1863.
CORVUS NORTHROP, Co. E, Dec. 28, 1861. See Obituary.
NATHAN PALMER, Co. E, Dec. 3, 1861. Discharged for disability Feb. 27, 1862.
CHARLES COUNCEL, Co. G, Dec. 5, 1861, re-enl. veteran, Jan. 1, 1864. He has a family here.
JOHN McCABE, Co. F, April 23, 1864.

THIRTEENTH.

COMPANY B.

JOHN J. HAIGHT, sergeant, Dec. 22, 1861, discharged for disability June 30, 1862, and re-enl. into the 6th Conn. Vol.
GEORGE H. PRATT, corporal, Jan. 11, 1862, re-enl. veteran, and commissioned 2d Lieut. May 1, 1864, and promoted 1st Lieut. Dec. 30, 1864. His name is on the roll of honor for meritorious service, June 14, 1862, at Port Hudson.
GEORGE W. TAYLOR, musician, Dec. 31, 1861.

ABRAHAM E. ACKLEY, Jan. 6, 1862.	See Obituary.
AARON S. AVERY, Jan. 11, 1862, discharged Jan. 14, 1863.
MARTIN BELL, Dec. 22, 1861, re-enl. veteran Feb. 8, 1864.
CLARK DIXON, Jan. 11, 1862, re-enl. vet., Feb. 8, 1864.
WILLIAM I. FERRIS, Feb. 10, 1862.	See Obituary.
THOMAS S. HARRIS, Feb. 27, 1862, discharged for disability June 30, 1862.
BANISTER H. JONES, March 5th, 1862, discharged for disability May 21, 1862.
JAMES R. KNAPP, Feb. 10, 1862, discharged for disability March 5, 1862.
EDWARD C. LOCKWOOD, Dec. 22, 1861.
GEORGE H. SEARLES, Jan. 18, 1862, discharged for disability June 30, 1862.
HENRY C. SEARLES, Feb. 18, 1862, discharged for disability July 5, 1862, and re-enl. into a N. Y. cavalry regiment.
JOHN ENNIS SEARLES, Jan. 6, 1862, was taken prisoner at Winchester.
GEORGE B. SELLECK, Dec. 22, 1861.	See Obituary.
BENJAMIN O. SEARLES, Feb. 26, 1862.	See Obituary.
JOHN J. TAYLOR, Dec. 22, 1861.	See Obituary.
JOHN W. THORNE, Feb. 20, 1862.	See Obituary.
JOSEPH THORNE, Feb. 10, 1862, re-enl. veteran Feb. 29, 1864, and was taken prisoner at Winchester, Sept. 19, 1864.
JOHN P. WEED, Dec. 31, 1861, wounded at Port Hudson, June 14, 1863.
BENJAMIN JONES, Co. H. Jan. 11, 1862.
EDWARD A. LOCKWOOD, Co. H, Jan. 11, 1862, discharged for disability Sept. 22, 1862.

EIGHTEENTH.

JOHN LILLEY, from Co. B, 2d Conn., was commissioned 2d Lieut. of Co. I, Oct. 19, 1863, in the 18th Conn. Promoted 1st Lieut. June 5, 1864, and Capt. Oct. 17, 1864, and was mustered out, June 27, 1865, after the war closed. In the spirited work done at Piedmont, Va., June

5, 1864, he was severely wounded in the leg. His family have been residing here since the war.

TWENTY-THIRD.

WILLIAM H. TROWBRIDGE, M. D., commissioned surgeon, Sept. 25, 1862, in the Banks' expedition, and taken prisoner near Brashear City. He was complimented with gift of sword, sash and belt from the citizens of the town. On his return from the South, was detailed surgeon of Board of Enrollment at Bridgeport, Conn., from which service he was discharged Aug. 31, 1863.

GEORGE BENEDICT, assistant surgeon, Jan. 22, 1863, and discharged Aug. 31, 1863.

HENRY H. ANDERSON, Co. I, Oct. 27, 1862, and honorably discharged Aug. 31, 1863. He re-enl. into the Navy.

TWENTY-FIFTH.

JOSEPH L. PEMBER, Co. K, Aug. 21, 1862, from Hartford; honorably discharged, Aug. 26, 1863, and is now living in Stamford.

TWENTY-SEVENTH.

ELISHA T. PAYNE, Co. C, Sept. 9, 1862, and honorably discharged July 27, 1863; has lived in Stamford since the war, in the practice of his profession as dentist.

TWENTY-NINTH.

JOSEPH FERMIN, Co. A, Nov. 28, 1863.

WILSON ESSEX, Co. B, Nov. 24, 1863.

STEPHEN GRAY, Co. B, Nov. 28, 1863.

ROBERT MITCHEL, Co. B, Jan. 4, 1864.

RICHARD MYERS, Co. B, Nov. 24, 1863.

GEORGE VANDIVERE, Co. B, Nov. 24, 1863.

WILLIAM NELLIS, Co. B, Dec. 4, 1863; was wounded severely in the elbow at Kell House, Virginia, Oct. 27, 27, 1864.

THOMAS L. BROWN, Co. G, Dec. 28, 1863.

ALLEN BANKS, Co. G, Jan 5, 1864; was shot in one leg at Fair Oaks.
JOHN BROWN, Co. G, Dec. 28, 1863.   See Obituary.
DAVID SNIVELY, Co. G, Dec. 28, 1863.
GEORGE E. BROWN, Sergt. Co. H, Dec. 31, 1863.
JOSEPH ELLIS, Co. H, Dec. 30, 1863.
WILLIAM H. BROWN, Co. H, Dec. 9, 1863, honorably discharged at Brownsville, Texas, October 24, 1865.
CHARLES E. TREADWELL, Co. H, Dec. 31, 1863.
RANDOLPH WILLIAMS, Co. H, Dec. 28, 1863.
ROBERT WILSON, Co. H, Dec. 30, 1863; reported deserter Feb. 5, 1864.
SIMON GREENE, Corp. Co. I, Jan. 4, 1864, discharged for disability June 27, 1864.
JOHN H. CLINE, Co. I, Jan. 1, 1864.
ABRAM LATTAN, Co. I, Jan. 5, 1864.
JOSIAH WALTON, Co. I, Jan. 4, 1864.
WILLIAM H. HAWKINS, Co. K, Jan. 4, 1864.
WILLIAM BANKS, April 20, 1864; reported deserting April 27, 1864.
DAVID JOHNSON, Co. H, June 2, 1864.
HENRY STARR, Dec. 9, 1863; reported as a deserter Jan. 7, 1864.

THIRTY-FIRST.

CHARLES E. ASIA, 1st Sergt. Co. B, Oct. 7, 1863.
JOSEPH HOOD, 1st Sergt. Co. D, Feb. 16, 1864.
JOHN H. SMITH, Corp. Co. D, Feb. 20, 1864.
JAMES W. YATES Co. D, Feb. 16, 1864, and mustered out at hospital, David's Island.

FIRST HEAVY ARTILLERY.

JEREMIAH O'RILEY, Co. C, May 23, 1861, discharged May 22, 1864, at end of term of service.
JAMES W. WEBB, Co. A, April 10, 1862.   See Obituary.
MICHAEL BURKE, Co. E, May 23, 1861, re-enl. Dec. 10, 1863.

JOSEPH D. PINKHAM, Co. C, May 23, 1861., re-enl. Nov. 16, 1863.

PATRICK BAKER, Co. K, May 23, 1861, is reported on Connecticut catalogue as a deserter. Sept. 7, 1861. He was afterwards in the Navy.

MORRIS CARROLL, May 23, 1861. See 10th Conn.

JAMES LIND, Co. K, May 23, 1861, reported deserter, Jan. 30, 1863.

JOHN MULHOLLAND, Co. K, May 23, 1861; and discharged May 22, 1864, on the expiration of his term of enlistment.

FRANCIS B. AVERY, Co. H, Nov. 30, 1863. See Obituary.
THEODORE BEDIENT, Co. H, Nov. 30, 1863.
SQUIRE S. BIRDSELL, Co. H, Nov. 28, 1863.
GEORGE W. FINCH, Co. H, Nov. 30, 1863.
WILLIAM FAGAN, Co. H, Nov. 30, 1863.
WILLIAM H. MONROE, Co. H, Dec. 8, 1863. See Obituary.
GEORGE H. POTT, Co. H, Nov. 28, 1863.
BENJAMIN SELLECK, Co. G, Dec. 7, 1863.
ELI STARR, Co. I, Jan. 4, 1864, from Hamden.

SECOND HEAVY ARTILLERY.

WILLIAM H. BREWER, Co. A, Jan. 2, 1864.
EZRA C. BOUTON, Co. C, Jan. 5, 1864. See Obituary.
EDGAR W. CONKLIN, Co. D, Dec. 30, 1863.
JOHN L. CONKLIN, Co. D, Dec. 30, 1863.
JOSEPH H. CANFIELD, Co. C, Jan. 5, 1864.
JAMES HENRY, Co. D, Jan. 1, 1864.
JACOB JUNE, Co. A, Jan. 14, 1864.
BANKS LOUNSBURY, Co. I, Jan. 28, 1864. See Obituary.
ALEXANDER MCCORMICK, Co. F, Jan. 18, 1864.
JOHN O'BRIEN, Co. B, Jan. 1, 1864.
SAMUEL S. OSBORN, Co. M, Feb. 11, 1864.
PATRICK RAIRDEN, Feb. 5, 1864, and discharged for disability, May 23, 1864.

CHAUNCEY STEVENS, Co. K, Jan. 5, 1864.
GEORGE TAYLOR, Co. C, Dec. 30, 1863.
JEREMIAH CONNER, Jan 5, 1864, from Bethel; has a family here.

SECOND LIGHT BATTERY.

ALLEN WEBB, Aug. 6, 1862, and discharged Aug. 9, 1865.
THOMAS CARROL, Feb. 18, 1864, to June 30, 1864.
MICHAEL DONNELLY, Feb. 18, 1864, to June 30, 1864.
PATRICK KELLEY, Feb. 18, 1864 to June 30, 1864.
ALONZO PECK, Jan. 5, 1864; reported in catalogue of Connecticut soldiers as a deserter, Jan. 19, 1864.
WILLIAM TAYLOR, Feb. 16, 1864, to June 30, 1864.
JAMES W. WELCH, Feb. 18, 1864, to June 30, 1864.

FIRST CAVALRY.

JAMES R. STRAIT, Sergt. Co. D, Nov. 2, 1861; re-enl. 2d Lieut. Jan. 2, 1864, promoted 1st Lieut. Feb. 26, 1664, and captain, Nov. 17, 1864, and mustered out Aug. 2, 1865.
MICHAEL CARRIGAN, Co. G, April 8, 1864.
DANIEL CONNER.
WARDELL HENDRICKS, Co. H, Dec. 8, 1863.
JOHN A. MCCLELLAN, Co. M, Dec. 30, 1863.
JAMES E. BISHOP, Co. D, Jan. 11, 1864.
WM. H. BISHOP, Co. E, Jan. 11, 1864, and discharged Aug. 20, 1865.

NEW YORK REGIMENTS.

HENRY V. SMITH, 1st Cavalry and re-enlisted into 12th Cavalry, serving about two years. While on a scouting expedition in Nov., 1864, near Plymouth, N. C., he was severely wounded by a ball which broke through the lower jaw, right side, and passing under the tongue came out under the left ear. He recovered, and is now in business in Danbury.
JAMES E. BISHOP, 1st Mounted Rifles, and re-enl. into 1st Conn. Cavalry.

ANTHONY MILLER, 2d State Militia.
RICHARD MORE, 2d State Militia.
HENRY PACKET, 2d State Militia.
PETER O'NEIL, 4th Heavy Artillery.
CHARLES W. KNAPP, 1st sergeant Co. B, 5th, Duryee's Zouaves, was taken prisoner at Savage Station, June 29, 1862. He was in prison until paroled, July 25, 1863; and for many months suffered severely from the confinement. He now resides in Hamden, Conn.
MATTHEW M. WALSH, Co. B, Duryee's Zouaves, and was taken prisoner at the second Bull Run fight, Aug. 31, 1862.
ALBERT SEAMAN was also in Duryee's Zouaves.
CHARLES W. SMITH served about three years in the Duryee's Zouaves, and is now living in Montana.
JAMES L. TAYLOR, Duryee's Zouaves. See Obituary.
WATSON B. NICHOLS, Duryee's Zouaves, April 19, 1861, and was in the fight at Great Bethel. He was mustered out May 18, 1863, after his term of service had expired. Re-enlisted Nov. 14, 1863, into Co. G, 1st Michigan Heavy Artillery. Appointed Hospital Steward Feb. 14, 1864, at Jackson, Miss. Transferred Aug. 31, 1864, as 2d lieutenant to 86th United States Infantry and promoted captain Oct. 12, 1865. He was appointed Provost Marshal and Judge Advocate for Southern District of Alabama. Resigned and was mustered out April 30, 1866. He has since his resignation been a student of medicine at Ann Arbor University.
THOMAS SKELDING, enlisted April 20, 1861, into Co. B, Duryee's Zouaves, and was chosen corporal. He was in the unfortunate engagement at Great Bethel. In Oct. of the same year he was commissioned captain Co. B, 10th New York McChesney's Zouaves, and resigned in Feb., 1862. He has, since leaving the service, graduated M. D., and is now in Europe on a professional visit to several prominent hospitals.
MICHAEL O'NEIL, Co. K, 5th Cavalry, Ira Harris Guard, re-enlisted veteran. He was wounded by a sabre stroke in the face, taken prisoner and from the sufferings of his

prison life has never recovered. He is now in a lunatic asylum.

DAVID H. SCOFIELD, Co. K, Ira Harris Guard. In a raid made by this famous cavalry, under Dalgreen, sergeant Scofield learned that General Henry A. Wise, of Virginia, was in the vicinity of their route, and made an attempt to capture him. From the published History of the Regiment, we take this account of the attempt : "He went to the place just as the redoubtable ex-governor mounted his horse. Scofield made after him, and quite an exciting chase ensued. The hero of Hatteras Island was not inclined to a personal encounter even with a single man, and being well mounted, succeeded in making his escape." In that ever memorable victory of Cedar Creek Oct. 19, 1864 the sergeant captured the colors of the 12th Virginia Infantry, for which gallant service he received a medal of honor, from the Secretary of War. It is on record respecting that battle: "among the regiments that participated in Sheridan's victory of Oct. 19th, none equaled the success of the Fifth New York Cavalry."

GEORGE W. TOMS, Co. K, Ira Harris Guard, Oct. 5, 1861, promoted commissary-sergeant in 1864, and returned home as 1st sergeant in July, 1865.

THEODORE NICHOLS, 6th Cavalry, 1861, and re-enlisted veteran. See Obituary.

WM. H. ROMER, 6th Heavy Artillery, and served three years. He came to Stamford in 1864, and now resides here.

JAMES W. DASKAM, on the opening of the war, promptly enlisted into the 7th National Guard.

HENRY H. HOLLY, Co. D, 7th National Guard. He has recently been appointed one of a committee of five from this famous regiment " on Plans and Construction," for erecting on Central Park a monument to those of its members who fell during the war.

WM. W. SMITH, National Guard.

JAMES R. WARREN, National Guard.

JOSEPH C. WARREN, National Guard.

M

WILLIAM POWELL, 8th N. Y. S. M.

GEO. A. YOUNGS, Co. K, 8th N. Y. Heavy Artillery.

HORACE GARDINER, 9th, Hawkins' Zouaves, 1861, and commissioned 2d lieutenant in 127th, Monitor Regiment, and promoted 1st lieutenant, serving about three years.

LEWIS GARDINER, Hawkins' Zouaves, 1861, commissioned 2d lieutenant in 127th, Monitor Regiment.

JOHN PARKER, Co. B, Hawkins' Zouaves, served two years.

WILLIAM PARKER, Hawkins' Zouaves.

JOHN HOYT, Hawkins' Zouaves and served two years.

EDGAR TOMS, Co. B, Hawkins' Zouaves, 1861, and served two years.

GEORGE TOMS, Co. B, Hawkins' Zouaves, 1861, was wounded at Antietam Sept. 11, 1862. He is now living here.

EDWARD KROLLPHEIFFER, Hawkins' Zouaves.

FREDERICK WARNER, Hawkins' Zouaves, went into the 64th New York, and still later was commissioned 2d lieutenant in the 10th Army Corps d'Afrique.

ALLEN CHAMBERLAIN, Co. I, 12th Cavalry in 1862, and re-enlisted into Navy.

Rev. P. S. EVANS, chaplain, 13th Heavy Artillery. See page 31.

WILLIAM J. WILSON, 17th Infantry.

CHARLES E. BETTS, 22d Infantry.
HIRAM TOTTEN, jr., 22d Infantry.
JAMES E. BOUTON, 22d Infantry.
WM. F. HALLOCK, 22d Infantry.
CHARLES SCOFIELD, 22d Infantry.
CHARLES WESTON, 22d Infantry.

WILLIAM NOLAN, 25th Infantry, 1861, was wounded, and is now in Ireland.

WILLIAM MCDONALD, 25th Infantry, 1861, and served twenty-six months.

OSCAR LASHER, 37th Infantry.

GEORGE LOCKWOOD, 38th Infantry, served twenty-five months.

MILITARY SERVICE.—NEW YORK REGIMENTS.

FREDERICK SHOWER, 39th Infantry, Garibaldi Guards, served three years.

SAMUEL M. PHYFE, Co. C, 47th Infantry, near Annapolis, Md.

JOHN SULLIVAN, 47th Infantry.

BRADFORD RAYMOND, Co. K, 48th Infantry, and served in the 5th Army Corps.

GEORGE FISH, 49th Infantry, was color bearer in the Army of the Potomac.

ALVA INGERSOL, 49th Infantry, was once wounded in the service.

CHARLES H. PALMER, 49th Infantry, and transferred with a captain's commission to the 6th New York Artillery. He was once wounded.

JOHN E. WEED, 49th Infantry, and re-enlisted veteran.

JOSEPH GIBSON, Co. K, 59th Infantry, then to 54th Infantry and then to 84th Ohio Infantry.

EDWIN R. DAILEY, Co. G, 67th Infantry.   See Obituary.

MICHAEL HANNAGAN, 69th Infantry.

JOHN W. MILLER, Company B, 71st Infantry, was called out to repel Lee's invasion in June 1863.

EDWARD A. QUINTARD, captain Co. B, New York National Guard, Engineer Corps, and was on guard duty in the vicinity of Washington. See Stamford History, page 407.

GEO. W. WEED, 71st Infantry, after three months service enlisted again into the 17th Conn.

WILLIAM E. WHITE, 90th Infantry.   See Obituary.

JOHN H. McDONALD, 82d New York.   See Obituary.

Rev. EBEN FRANCIS, chaplain, 127th, Monitor. See page 32.

EDWARD OLDRIN, 127th, Monitor, and after serving about sixteen months was discharged for disability.

THEODORE MILLER, from 10th Connecticut, re-enlisted into Co. A, 139th New York Volunteers. He was commissioned lieutenant Sept. 9, 1862, promoted captain March 9, 1863, and major Oct. 14, 1864. He was appointed colonel in the Corps d'Afrique April 12, 1865, but did not muster. As soldier and officer he has a creditable record.

FRANKLIN A. JONES, served in Scott's Life Guard.

BENJAMIN R. SAUNDERS, was in a New York Heavy Artillery regiment.

JOHN HANFORD, was successively in two regiments of New York.

JAMES MCCARTY, left the employ of the Phœnix Company and enlisted in a New York regiment, and served two years.

JOHN H. SEARLES, was in a New York regiment.

HENRY C. SEARLES, from 13th Conn. went into a New York Cavalry regiment.

REGIMENTS OF OTHER STATES.

JAMES R. AYRES, Co. C, 3d Michigan.   See Obituary.

FREDERICK BISHOP, 5th New Jersey Battery, was discharged for disability.

HANFORD BISHOP, 5th New Jersey Battery.

JOHN CARROL, Co. A, 32d Ohio, Nov. 22, 1864, from Toledo. He served to the end of the war when he came to Stamford with his family.

SAMUEL FESSENDEN was mustered into the service of the United States, March 3, 1864, at sixteen years of age, as a private in 7th Maine Battery, 1st Regiment Light Artillery. He was appointed 1st lieutenant 2d Regiment United States Infantry, Dec. 14, 1864, and captain of Infantry, Dec. 20, 1864. His bravery, good conduct in battle, and fitness to command had attracted the notice of his superior officers, and having been warmly recommended for a commission in the artillery service, he declined promotion in the infantry. He was commissioned 2d lieutenant, 1st Battery, Maine Light Infantry, Jan. 18, 1865, and detailed to the staff of major-general A. P. Howe, May 1, 1865, serving in that position till the close of the war. At the battles of the Wilderness, Spotsylvania, North and South Anna, Cold Harbor, Petersburg, Weldon R. R., The Mine Explosion, Reams Station,

Poplar Grove Church, and Hatcher's Run, he did good service, receiving the universal commendations of his superior officers in every position in which he served. He was admitted to the Fairfield County Bar, March 4, 1869, and is now completing his legal studies at Harvard Law School. The family have resided in Stamford since 1866.

PHILO C. FULLER, 2d Illinois Volunteers.   See Obituary.

EMMET M. HOYT, 3d Maryland and also in a New York regiment.   See Obituary.

SAMUEL C. INGERSOLL, 3d Maryland, was wounded at Antietam and discharged.

PETER HURD, 14th Rhode Island Heavy Artillery, Oct. 14, 1863.

JAMES KEEGAN, Co. K, 18th Kentucky, in 1864, and came to Stamford at the end of the war.

JOSEPH S. LOCKWOOD, 141st Penn.   See Obituary.

RICHARD PIERSON, 3d Maryland.

WILLIAM E. SCOFIELD, 74th Illinois.   See Obituary.

GEORGE VANDERVALDT, 1st Reserve Cavalry, Pennsylvania. See Obituary.

PIERRE R. HOLLY, M. D., appointed assistant surgeon in the spring of 1863, and assigned to the Douglas Hospital, Washington City. After the Gettysburg battles, he was assigned to the 22d Wisconsin Infantry, and remained in the service until discharged at his request in the spring of 1864. Having, previously to the war, practiced in the West Indies and in Greenwich, Conn., he settled here in his profession in 1866.

The following citizens of the town were in the service of the Government, though not connected with any particular regiment:

GEORGE E. BADGER, M. D., who left his practice here, with a commission as contract surgeon, and was stationed at David's Island.

John Davenport was aid to colonel John H. Almy, assistant-quarter-master-general of Connecticut, and stationed at New York for supplying the Connecticut and Rhode Island volunteers.

John C. Mixor, M. D., commissioned, April 1, 1863, acting assistant surgeon, U. S. A., after having voluntarily served on Hospital Ships of the Sanitary Commission during the preceding year. Was in the Army of Cumberland until Feb. 3, 1864, when he was ordered to Harrisburg, Penn., to take charge of Port Hospital. He resigned Oct. 4, 1864.

Rev. J. H. Parks, commissioned chaplain, July 5, 1862, and assigned to Carver Hospital, Washington City. See Stamford History, page 327.

John T. Riley was acting quarter-master at Washington City and elsewhere.

Samuel C. Staples, assistant paymaster U. S. A.

Hennel Stevens entered the service as medical purveyor at Cairo, Ills., in 1862, and was ordered to Memphis in May, 1865. The testimony to his good service is abundant. The Memphis *Daily Commercial* at the close of the war said of him: "He deserves well of the Department. He has displayed not only tact and skill but all the qualities of patient endurance so necessary to a fair performance of duty." At the close of the war he purchased a plantation in Texas for cultivation.

UNITED STATES ARMY.

David C. Comstock, Jr., from Co. H, 17th Conn., entered Jan. 9, 1864, the United States Army as hospital steward. He was first ordered to Louisville, Ky., and then to New Albany, Illinois. He was next sent to forts Selden and Cummings, in New Mexico. At all of these posts he rendered valuable service, and continued, until his health failing, he was obliged to leave. He was honorably discharged, Jan. 31, 1867. He has since been a student in medicine, at Ann Arbor, Mich., and in the Bellevue Medical College, of New York City.

GEORGE W. CHAMBERLAIN, from Co. B, 17th Conn. Vol., enlisted into a regiment of the U. S. Cavalry, Feb. 3, 1863.

PATRICK FARREL, enlisted in 1859 in the regular U. S. Army He had one of his legs broken at Petersburg, Va., where he was struck by nine balls.

SAMUEL B. FERRIS, educated at West Point, class of 1861, graduated 2d lieutenant, and assigned to the 8th U. S. Inf. He was with his regiment at the first Bull Run rout of June 21, 1861, and until his commission as Colonel of the 28th Conn. Vol. On the expiration of his commission he returned to his regiment as 1st Lieut., until transferred with captain's commission to the 20th U. S. Infantry. In 1867, he was ordered with his regiment to the Indian country on the North West, and is now stationed at Fort Saunders, Wyoming Territory.

FRANCIS M. HOLLY, appointed assistant surgeon in the winter of 1862, and assigned to Hospital at Portsmouth, opposite Norfolk, Va. He resigned in 1863, and returned to the practice of his profession. In 1868 he was appointed surgeon in the United States Army, and is now with his regiment at Belton, Texas.

JOHN L. HOYT, Co. B., 1st U. S. Reg. Art., Nov. 4, 1862, from which, at the expiration of his term of enlistment, he was discharged Sept. 5, 1864. In this arm of the service, he was in sixteen severe engagements. In the raid in Florida from the 7th to the 17th of Feb., 1864, as his discharge testifies, he traveled 780 miles, and in Virginia, from the 20th to the 30th of June, 696 miles. He was once knocked from his horse by a ball while in action, and had two horses shot under him.

WILLIAM P. JONES, on the opening of the war, as our record of the Citizen Service shows, promptly tendered his services to the Government. He was appointed aid-de-camp on the staff of Major-General John E. Wool, April 24, 1861, with rank of colonel of volunteers. He rendered valuable service in New York, in the spring and summer of 1861, to the Union Aid Committee. Sept. 20, 1861, he was appointed aid-de-camp, with the rank of major in the regular army, and ordered to report to Gen. Wool. In this capacity, he served at Fortress Monroe, Va. He was appointed Provost Marshal, Gen. of the Dept. of Virginia, and assisted at the taking of Yorktown and Norfolk. On the removal of General Wool, in 1862, to Baltimore, he was appointed Mil. Pro. Mar. of the Mid. Dept., embracing Maryland, Pennsylvania and New Jersey. He was very active and efficient in organizing the aid of negroes in the war. His health at length gave way, and he resigned, though not before he had earned "for gallant and meritorous service." his commission of brevet brig.-general of volunteers, dating from March 13, 1865. Few of our citizens sacrificed as much in leaving business to enter the service of the government as General Jones, as none had entered into the support of the war more heartily than he.

JOHN MANNING, June 16, 1860, 3d U. S. Cavalry, in which arm of the service he continued until July 14, 1867, when he was honorably discharged. He was a sergeant in his company, and at Memphis was orderly on the staff of General Grant, and afterwards was orderly to General Sherman. He is now living here.

HENRY O'NEIL, Co. B, 5th U. S. infantry, early in the war, and still remains in the service.

ALBERT M. POWELL.   See Obituary.

HENRY ROCKWELL, M. D., surgeon in the U. S. Army. On leaving the 28th Conn. Vol. he was stationed a while at Fort Schuyler. He is now on duty at Fort Totten, Dacota Territory.

JAMES SCOFIELD, in 1859 entered the U. S. Army, and was assigned to the 4th regiment of infantry.

EDWIN L. SMITH, Sept. 2, 1864, was transferred from the 17th Conn. Vol. to Co. A, 9th U. S. Reserves. He was taken prisoner in Florida.

FRANCIS L. STILL, Oct. 13, 1863, transferred from 6th Conn. Vol. to Signal Corps in the U. S. Army.

WILLIAM J. SLOAN, of Pennsylvania, appointed assistant

surgeon in the U. S. Army, 1837. Served in Florida
during the Seminole war, 1837–40; in the Choctaw
country west of Arkansas, at Forts Towson and Washita,
from 1840 to 1841; stationed in Philadelphia in 1845;
next year ordered to New Orleans, where, and at Baton
Rouge he remained until 1849, when he was sent again to
Florida until 1853. In 1856 promoted surgeon, and
ordered to New Mexico, holding the position of medical
director, Department of New Mexico, until 1860. After
four months' leave of absence, he was assigned to duty at
Governor's Island, New York harbor, where the opening
of the rebellion found him. Was then ordered to New
York City as Supt. of Hospitals. Under his supervision
the Transport Service was organized, and provision made
for patients from the seat of war. As assistant medical
director of the department, he also aided in organizing
twenty-eight general hospitals in New England, New York
and New Jersey, which comprised in all twenty-five
thousand beds. In 1862 he was ordered to Minnesota as
medical director of the department of the North-West,
but was in a few months returned to his post in New
York, where he subsequently became medical director of
the department until the close of the war. The number
of sick and wounded soldiers cared for in this department
during his term of service, was about one hundred and
fifty thousand. For his services thus rendered, he was
successively brevetted lieutenant-colonel, colonel and
brigadier general. He still continues in New York on
duty, as chief medical officer, with the usual routine of
duties in time of peace, his residence being, as for several
years, in Stamford.

DAVID H. VINTON, graduated at West Point, 1822, entering
the U. S. A. as lieutenant in the Artillery service. He
had been in various branches of the service, as an efficient
officer both in time of peace and of war; until the war of
1861–5 found him chief quartermaster of the Department
of Texas, headquarters, San Antonio, where he was taken
prisoner by the rebels and paroled. During our war for
the suppression of the rebellion, he has rendered impor-

tant services to the Government. He was colonel in the Volunteer Army from Aug. 2, 1864, to July 29, 1866. Chief quartermaster at New York City, for supplying the army with clothing and equipage from June 28, 1861, to July, 1867, (ex-officio). Brevet brigadier general U. S. Army, March 13, 1865, and brevet major general U. S. Army, March 13, 1865, for faithful and meritorious services during the rebellion. He was retired from active service, July 29, 1866, and now resides on the corner of North street and Adams Avenue.

JAMES WRIGHT, U. S. Army, Feb. 22, 1863, but to what arm of the service is not known.

MILITARY SERVICE. 107

The following citizens, being liable to service, some of whose names have already appeared on our list as having rendered good service in the field, sent also, substitutes or paid the commutation. Probably some of them are represented on our previous lists of recruits, though many of their substitutes were assigned to unknown regiments. For other substitutes, not legally required, see pages 33 and 34. The names of the substitutes would have been added but for the impossibility of getting them:

John Davenport,
Theo. Davenport,
Alex. H. Weed,
Frank Hoyt,
Hiram Curtis,
Charles H. Brown,
George L. Warren,
Otto Loeschigk,
John Day Ferguson,
Samuel Ferguson,
Andrew Stark,
Lewis R. Hurlbutt,
Charles P. Holmes,
Oliver Hoyt,
Samuel H. Holmes,
Edward F. Leeds,
Charles W. Wardwell,

John St. John,
Wm. W. Skiddy,
William C. Willcox,
Samuel B. Hoyt,
James Smith,
Dwight Waugh,
Charles W. Hoyt,
Charles H. Holly,
Cyrus D. Jones,
Isaac S. Jones,
John H. Brush,
Charles W. Brown,
Robert B. Scofield,
Elbert June,
George P. Waterbury,
Robert Swartwout,
Satterlee Swartwout.

The following citizens, upon being drafted, supplied substitutes:

James B. Davenport,
James H. Olmstead,
Walter Ferguson,
Alexander Raeburn,
Joseph E. Lockwood,
Edward F. Brown,
John Rosborough,
Edward Hannagan,
Edward Kennady,

Charles M. Scofield,
Edgar S. Weed,
Chauncey Provost,
E. S. Gifford,
Leroy Scofield,
Charles J. Smith,
Alonzo Stevens,
R. S. Miller,
Charles E. Thompson.

For special and very delicate, as well as difficult service rendered the Government during the war, we should here record the name and official position of Wm. T. Minor, L.L.D., ex-governor of the State. It is due equally to himself and to our town to add to his citizen service. See Part I, his official services, also, as Consul General at Havana. Though not to be traced out, as the march and conquest of an army, it is still true that his services in diplomacy while at Havana were as important to our cause, as victories on the battle field. On leaving his post, he was honored by very abundant and flattering official testimonials to his successful mission. See Stamford History, p. 376.

PART THIRD.

NAVAL SERVICE.

NAVAL SERVICE.

The following catalogue contains the list of those who rendered good service to the Government of the United States in the Navy during the war. Many a gallant deed was performed by these representatives of the town which history will never report.

WILLIAM D. ADAMS, April 3, 1862, as boy, and in two months promoted landsman.

HENRY H. ANDERSON, Sept. 1863, landsman and served one year.

S. L. P. AYRES, appointed assistant engineer in 1858, making his first cruise in the Roanoke, the Flag Ship of the Home Squadron. In 1860, assigned to duty in Brooklyn Navy Yard. In March, 1861, ordered to Lake duty on the Michigan; and soon transferred to the Frigate Pensacola, in Farragut's expedition against New Orleans. Was in the engagements at forts Philip and Jackson and present at the surrender of New Orleans. Was promoted chief engineer and assigned to the Nipsic, on blockade duty off Charleston. Assigned next, in 1865, to the Juniata as her chief, and ordered to the Brazilian waters, and, in 1867, ordered to Portsmouth Navy Yard as inspecting engineer, where he is still on duty. He made a good record for himself during the war. In the engagement of April 25, 1862, on the Mississippi, he boarded a rebel man-of-war and brought off with him the rebel colors, as one trophy of his prowess.

PATRICK BAKER, Sept. 1, 1863, a seaman.

CHARLES H. BRANTINGHAM, at the opening of the war was on the last year of his course at the Naval Academy, Annapolis, Md. He was ordered to the Somerset, March 10, 1862, as navigator and drill officer, from which he was sent as drill master to the two ships Amanda and Hendrick Hudson, from which he returned as navigator to the Somerset, and promoted ensign. He was then promoted to command the Icilda, and subsequently was connected with the Cherokee and Honduras, and in command of the Sunflower. He saw the beginning of his service as a detail to protect the Constitution, in Annapolis Roads, 1861. He was in several sharp engagements, and successful in taking several prizes the Circassian, the Curlew, the Hortense. In June 1865, ordered to the Winooski, at the Dock trial of the Winooski and Algonquin in New York. Promoted master, July 3, 1865, and ordered to N. Y. Navy Yard, Jan. 17, 1866. An incident in his service is a good illustration of his personal character and spirit. He had been ordered while on the Appilachicola to reconnoiter in citizen's dress. He demanded the order in writing, and when he had secured it, he coolly informed his commander that he should obey no such order, though he would cheerfully volunteer the service in his uniform. As witness to his readines to dare, when duty called, he still has a rebel flag which he personally captured at Appilachicola. He resigned his commission, April 18, 1867, and is in business in New York.

PETER CAVANOUGH, 1st quartermaster, March 2, 1863.

ALLEN CHAMBERLAIN, May 17, 1864, landsman.

PETER CONROY, May 8, 1864, landsman.

CHARLES I. DAYTON, Aug. 7, 1862, landsman in the East Gulf Squadron.

DAVID DECKER, master's mate in Burnside expedition, 1862.

PETER DECKER, master's mate in Porter's Morter Fleet, 1862.

JAMES DELAMATER, Aug. 10, 1862, seaman.

CORNELIUS DEVER, July 20, 1864, seaman.

RICHARD DEVER, Oct., 1863, landsman and promoted seaman.

NAVAL SERVICE. 113

DANIEL DILLON, Sept. 9, 1862, seaman, and again Sept. 20, 1864.
RICHARD DILLON, Oct., 1863.
DAVID R. DREW, June, 1864, the second time, ship Saratoga.
GEO. A. EBBETTS, captain's clerk, April, 1864, and sailed in June on the Bienville. In the action in Mobile Bay, Aug. 1864, he is reported by lieutenant Huntington, of the Oneida, to which he had volunteered for more active service as being very courageous. Though knocked down, at the same time that his captain was wounded, he rallied himself, and with the utmost coolness, in the midst of whizzing death shots, ministered to the needs of the wounded.
ISIDORE FERRIS, captain's clerk, May 1, 1864.
BENJAMIM F. FRENCH, May 16, 1864, first class boy.
THOMAS FOX, July 15, 1861, first class boy and promoted landsman.
JOHN GAGAN, from 28th Conn. Vol., Sept. 1, 1863, landsman.
LEWIS GARDNER.
JOSEPH GARDNER.
CHAS. H. TAYLOR, master's mate, Dec. 23, 1863, and assigned to the Proteus.
JOSEPH GIBSON served one year.
JAMES H. GIBLIN, Aug, 11, 1864.
GEO. W. GLENDINING, paymaster's clerk, Feb. 1, 1864.
THEODORE M. HALLOCK, Dec. 16, 1863, landsman one year.
FRANCIS M. HAWLEY, Act.-Ass.-Paymaster, Aug. 30, 1862, and assigned to the Carondelet, at Cairo, Ills.
ALBERT HOBBY, served a year with captain John Ketchum.
THEODORE HOBBY.
JOHN M. HOLLY, Aug. 9, 1862, landsman and discharged Sept. 9, 1863.
GEORGE HUDSON, Aug. 10, 1862, seaman.
SAMUEL H. JOHNSON, entered the Navy, Nov. 9, 1860, ap-

pointed acting master's mate, Oct. 31, 1861, on Suwanee. He was later in command of bark Midnight, and received his discharge, Dec. 23, 1865.

MARTIN KANE, Sept. 9, 1862, landsman.

DANIEL KENNEDY, seaman in 1861.

DENNIS KENNEDY, May, 1862, seaman.

JOHN KETCHAM, assistant master's mate, and acting master in the Potomac Flotilla.

JOHN KILEY.

HENRY K. LAPHAM, a native of Stamford, acting master mate, Oct. 3, 1861, assigned during the war to the Suwanee.

ZOPHAR LAWRENCE, sailed with captain Ketcham.

HENRY LEE, Feb., 1862, seaman on the Matthew Vassar.

JOHN LEONARD, June 7, 1861, and re-enl., 1865, landsman.

GEORGE LLOYD, Sept. 1, 1863, seaman.

ALBERT L. LOCKWOOD, Feb., 1862, seaman.

WM. B. LUM, Dec. 23, 1863, first class boy.

MICHAEL MANAHAN, April, 1864, seaman.

PATRICK MCKEON, 1862.

AUGUSTUS F. MILLER, Sept 19, 1861, acting master's mate.

JOHN M. NEWMAN, Act. 3d Ass. Engineer Sept. 3, 1864.

EDWARD F. NICHOLS, from 3d Conn. Vol., Oct. 28, 1864, ship Chippewa.

PETER O'NEIL, 1861, on Oneida in the Gulf, and afterwards went into the Cavalry Service.

HENRY O'NEIL.

PETER RANKIN, Feb. 14, 1862, as boy, and promoted landsman.

JAMES H. ROWAN, May 27, 1864, honorary seaman.

GEORGE A. SCOFIELD, Sept. 10, 1862, U. S. Marine Corps for four years; taken prisoner by the Alabama in the Caribbean sea in 1863.

JOHN O. SCOFIELD, served first as medical steward in hospitals in Virginia. In 1866 was with the U. S. Squadron which visited Europe, and is now a practicing physician in Bedford, New York.

WALTER K. SCOFIELD, assistant surgeon, June 20, 1861, and promoted surgeon in 1866. During the war was in various hospitals in Boston, New York, Norfolk, Key West, Pensacola, and New Orleans; was at the bombardment of Sumpter, capture of Appalachicola, and on blockading service at Galveston and Mobile. Was surgeon of the squadron which visited Europe in 1866, making the tour of Russia, Sweden, Prussia, England, and Italy. He now has his headquarters in Boston.

HOBBY SELLECK, July 2, 1864, seaman. See Obituary.

FREDERICK SHOWER was reported in the naval service.

ROBERT W. SHUFELDT dates his service in the U. S. navy from May 11, 1839. In March, 1861, he was appointed Consul-General to Cuba, and was the right man for the office when our recent war opened. He re-entered the Navy as commander, in May, 1863, and was assigned to the steamer Proteus, his commission dating from Nov. 19, 1862. He served one year off Charleston, and participated in the capture of Morris Island. He had, later, command on the West coast of Florida, and co-operated with our gun-boats in the attack by the army on St. Marks, one of the last actions of the war.

ROBERT SHUFELDT, Jr., April 9, 1863, captain's clerk on the Proteus.

HENRY T. SKELDING, Dec. 31, 1862, acting assistant paymaster, and assigned to the Petrel at Cairo; commissioned passed assistant paymaster, March 5, 1867, and is now on waiting orders.

JAMES SNIFFIN, Aug. 7, 1862, landsman, and re-enl. Aug. 17, 1864, 2d class fireman one year.

CLARK STEVENS, July 20, 1864, as boy, and promoted seaman.

HENRY STEINART.

HENRY STOTTLAR, Dec. 1861, seaman. See Obituary.

CHARLES J. TODD, April 11, 1863, assistant paymaster, U. S. steamer Shockokon, serving through the war.

ANDREW WALTER, Dec. 18, 1863, landsman on the Hartford.

JAMES W. WATERBURY, June 30, 1864, screw steamer Hartford, at the capture of Fort Morgan, Mobile Bay, and continuing in the service until February, 1868.

JAMES WEED, first-class firemen, Nov. 14, 1862.

JAMES WELCH, Aug. 24, 1862, landsman.

GEORGE E. WHITNEY, June 2, 1862, assistant engineer on the Mohawk, taken prisoner in Florida, May 3, 1864, and paroled in October, same year.

HERCULES WICKS, 28 years old, Jan. 1, 1862, on the flag ship of Burnside's expedition.

M. B. WOOLSEY, son of Commodore Woolsey, entered the U. S. Navy Sept. 24, 1832, and commissioned commander July 16, 1861. Before the war he had been for some time retired from duty, having been greatly reduced by the fever, taken while on duty on the African coast. At his own request he was assigned again to duty early in the war, and in 1865 he was reported in command of the Princess Royal. He is now fleet captain in the South American Squadron.

EDWARD YOUNGS, Dec. 2, 1862, as first-class boy and became seaman.

WILLIAM D. WHITING, entered the navy March 1, 1841, as midshipman, and was past-midshipman 1848. The opening of the recent war found him lieutenant on the North Carolina, receiving ship. On the occasion of the temporary blockade of railroad transit through Baltimore, he was attached to the brig Perry, to convoy troops to Annapolis. As executive officer, he was attached to the Vandalia, on blockade duty off South Carolina, and was in the Port Royal engagements. He was promoted lieutenant commander July 16, 1862, and attached to the Wyandot, and still later to the Ottawa off Charleston. Near the close of the war he was attached to the school ship Savannah, for instruction of volunteer officers, and stationed in New York harbor. He was also assigned to the gun-boat Tioga, of the gulf squadron. He has been for some time attached to the navy-yard duty at New York. His family have resided here since 1865.

PART FOURTH.

OBITUARY.

OBITUARY.

It is specially fitting that our MEMORIAL should prove a worthy monument to the memory of our dead. We owe it ourselves to honor those who so cheerfully gave themselves for our cause. Let us, then, here affectionately enroll the names of these, our departed, where they shall be to us a perpetual witness to the self-sacrificing loyalty of those whom we have lost. While this brief necrology shall often start the tear from the eye of many a stricken mourner who still misses some dear one, lost, let it, also, kindle to a holier earnestness, a love for the great cause they died to save. May it never cease to inspire in our hearts, too, the same pure and grand devotion, which shall so honor and hallow forever the memories of these our dead.

> So passed the strong, heroic soul away.
> TENNYSON.
>
> Fallen are the faithful and the pure.
> MRS. HEMANS.
>
> They fought to give us peace, and lo!
> They gained a better peace than ours.
> PHEBE CAREY.
>
> Forget them not, though now their names
> Be but a mournful sound.
> MRS. HEMANS.

ABRAHAM E. ACKLEY, Co. B, 13th Conn., son of widow Mary Ackley, is reported in the Catalogue of Connecticut Soldiers as having died, Aug. 9, 1863.

FRANCIS B. AVERY, a recruit from Stamford, Co. H, First Conn. Artillery, though residing in Poundridge. He is reported as having died, March 12, 1864.

JAMES R. AYRES, son of Jeremiah N. Ayres, Co. C, 3d Michigan. He entered the regiment at twenty years of age, and was found at his post with his regiment, on the march and in action, down to the day of his fall, June 17, 1864, before Petersburg. The following from the treasurer of the Michigan Soldiers' Relief Association, bearing the same date, tells the story of his death.

"Twenty minutes ago, your son James R. Ayres, while laboring on the breastworks, about fifty feet from brigade headquarters, fell, shot through the left breast by a rebel sharpshooter. He expired within two minutes, without uttering a word. He has been buried under a locust on the bank of a small stream, forty rods north of a road leading east of Petersburg, and a mile or two from that city. I understand he was a gallant soldier and much esteemed in his regiment." He left a good name and his memory is held very precious to his friends, who are thus called to mourn so early his death.

THADDEUS L. BAILEY, Co. C, 28th Conn., son of John L. Bailey, died of fever at Memphis, Sept. 16, 1863, about three weeks after his discharge, leaving a wife and one daughter.

NATHANIEL BARMORE, jr., son of Nathaniel, Co. B, 28th Conn., returned broken down by the campaign, and died here of chronic diarrhea. He left a wife and children.

JOHN E. BING, Co. D, 6th Conn., was one of the three

sons of Mrs. Mary A. Bing who were in the service. He was the first of his company to yield to the hardships and privations of the campaign, in South Carolina. He died of fever, April 8, 1862, in the hopital at Hilton Head, at a time when the sanitary provisions of the army were insufficient to meet the wants of the wounded and the sick.

JOHN BOUAN, a recruit for Co. I, 10th Conn., who is supposed to have been killed at the Deep Run engagement. He was a single man.

EZRA B. BOUTON, Co. C, 2d Artillery Conn. Volunteers, was son of Stephen Bouton. He was killed at Cold Harbor, June 3, 1864, and left a wife and four children.

JOHN E. BOUTON, Co. A, 28th Conn., son of Nathaniel A. Bouton. He died, Sept. 29, 1863, in Baton Rouge hospital, from typhoid fever, at twenty-eight years of age. His record was a good one, and his death was keenly felt by his comrades, whose confidence and esteem he had won.

SPENCER BOUTON, Co. A, 28th Conn., son of Joseph Bouton. He was left in the hospital at Brashear City, with eighteen other sick soldiers of the regiment, May 23, 1863, as the regiment started up the river. He died, there, on the 7th of the following month. He was a victim, doubtless, to the miserable quarters which our soldiers found on the muddy flats of that locality. He left a wife and two children.

ANDREW BOYD, Sergt. Co. B, 28th Conn., a native of New York City, was here, in the firm of Lockwood & Boyd, when the war began. While in service in the Mississippi Valley, he was attacked with chronic diarrhea, and though able to reach home, he could not be helped. His death occurred, Oct. 5, 1863, at the age of forty-five. He was an exemplary citizen and a good soldier. His funeral was attended by his pastor, Rev. E. Francis, from the Universalist church, and his remains were interred in the Northfield burying lot. He left a wife and five children.

PHINEAS BROWN, Co. H, 28th Conn., son of widow Harrison Brown, was living in the Turn of the River district on the opening of the war. He came home sick from the South, and died, Sept. 6, 1863, unmarried.

JOHN BROWN, Co. G, 29th Conn., was killed in the action near Kell House, Oct. 27, 1864, while the company was working their way through the picket lines up to the enemy's entrenchments. The action continued from seven A. M. until the morning of the next day.

FRANK BRYSON, Co. D, 6th Conn., was wounded severely in the breast, May 15, 1864, near Bermuda Hundred, and died from the wounds at Point Lookout, May 19th. His record is that of a good soldier, and when his misfortune took him into the hospital, he was found a faithful and useful nurse. It is due that this misfortune be stated. In the fall of 1863, he came home on his furlough for a visit. Taken sick, he could not return according to his furlough, and was reported a deserter. On his return he was tried and acquitted, but his health not being equal to the field, he was transferred to the hospital, where his help was found very serviceable. He left a wife and children here.

JOHN BUTTRY, Co. B, 17th Conn., was one of those taken prisoner at Welaka, Fla., May 19, 1864. He was taken to Andersonville, where it is probable he died, though no reliable report of his death has ever been received. His family have lived a year or two in Darien.

SAMUEL CALDWELL, Co. B, 28th Conn., son of George;

was taken with the fever while on the Mississippi river, and brought to Fort Schuyler, where he died Aug. 15, 1863. His remains were interred in the burying ground at the Turn of the River.

MORRIS CARROLL, Co. G, 10th Conn., wounded at Drury's Bluff, May 13, 1864. Both hands were badly shattered, and he refused to have them amputated. He died in the hospital in New Haven, July 28, 1864, aged nineteen.

JOHN S. CLARK, Corp. Co. D, 6th Conn., son of John Clark, and born in New York City in 1844. The family had been living here several years when the war began, and he was one of our earliest volunteers. After serving out his first term honorably, he as cheerfully re-enlisted, and in the thirteenth battle in which he was engaged, he was killed, probably by a sharpshooter, Aug. 16, 1864, at Strawberry Plains. His record as a soldier was one of our best; and the high esteem in which he was held was fully deserved. No report was received of him after the action in which he fell. Thus died this patriot youth at the early age of seventeen.

EDWARD T. CLARK, son of Levi Clark, Co. B, 28th Conn., was sent May 25, 1863, to the hospital at Baton Rouge, where he died Aug. 17, 1865.

GEORGE W. CLOCK, Co. A, 28th Conn., died at the Baton Rouge, La., Hospital, July 2, 1863.

LEWIS A. COOK, Co. E, 7th Conn., proved himself to be a good soldier. In the severe fighting at Deep Run, Va., Aug. 16, 1864, he was especially commended by his captain, John Thompson, then commanding the regiment. Again in the difficult advance of Oct. 27th of the same year, led by General Butler, on the Darbytown road, his bravery and good judgment were conspicuous, and for these he was urgently recommended by Butler for promotion.

ANDREW CRISSY, Co. B, 28th Conn., died at Brashear City Hospital, after having been honorably discharged with his regiment, Aug. 26, 1863.

EDWIN R. DAILY, Co. G, 67th N. Y. Vols., was a native of Michigan, and step-son of John Clark, Esq., of Stamford. He first volunteered with the men who afterwards constituted Co. D, 6th Conn., but not willing to wait for the regimental organization, he enlisted as above. After brave service in nineteen engagements, he fell in his twentieth, in the battle of the Wilderness, May 6, 1864, twenty-three years of age. He was struck by the ball of a sharpshooter, as he stood about about six yards in advance of his comrades, he cheering them on to the fight. His honorable record is, " he fell a true Christian patriot."

JOHN W. DASKAM, son of Mrs. Betsy Daskam, went out with the 6th Conn., as cook, and was taken with the fever in Beaufort, N. C., where he died early in October, 1862, aged thirty years. He had made himself useful to the regiment, and his death was felt to be a great loss to them.

CHARLES DURAND, Co. B, 28th Conn., had been residing in Stamford for a few years, and when he volunteered was engaged as keeper of the Cornucopia Restaurant. He was a resolute and courageous soldier and officer. One of the detail for the assault on Port Hudson, of June 14, 1864, he fell almost immediately on the sounding of the charge, while urging on his men. His remains were recovered under a flag of truce, and buried near the picket fence.

WILLIAM FARNOLD, Co. B, 17th Conn., son of William, of Greenwich; was taken prisoner at Welaka, May 19, 1864, and confined in Andersonville. On his exchange he was so

OBITUARY.   125

completely reduced by the treatment, to which, as a Union
soldier, he had been subjected, that he did not reach home.
At Wilmington, N. C., March 19, 1865, death released him
from what could only have been a life of lingering suffering for
him. His family were awaiting his arrival with affectionate
longings, only to be thrice disappointed. Within five weeks
of his death, his two only children died here, one of five, and
the other of three years of age, leaving the wife alone, thus
widowed and childless. He was twenty-five years old.

GEORGE D. FERRIS, Co. B, 17th Conn., son of John and Jane
Feeks. After being taken a prisoner at Welaka, Florida,
he was sent from one southern prison to another, until at
Florence he contracted the disease of which he died May
1865, at the Navy Hospital, Annapolis, Md. He left a wife
and one child. The child is now in Fitch's Soldiers' Home.

WILLIAM I. FERRIS, Co. B, 13th Conn., died May 9, 1863,
of fever, in hospital at the South.

MICHAEL FOX, Co. B, 17th Conn., was shot in the first
charge made upon his company at Gettysburg, July 1, 1863.
He left a wife and three children who are still living here.

PATRICK FOX, Co. D, 6th Conn., went into the engagement
near Bermuda Hundred, June 17, 1864. He was taken
prisoner, and is reported as dying, Nov. 6, 1864, leaving a
family.

DANIEL FREEMAN, Co. D, 6th Conn., died July 12, 1862,
on Dawfaskie Island, after a short sickness of one week.

PETER FRYLINGHUM, Co. B, 28th Conn., is reported on the
company record by the Adjutant-General of the State, as
discharged for disability, Jan. 19, 1863. I find no record of
his death, which occurred in Stanwich, but his daughter
Louisa is returned by the selectmen, as entitled to the benefit

of the "Act for the relief of soldiers' children," in September, 1866.

PHILO C. FULLER, son of S. B. Fuller, of New York City; enlisted into the 20th Ill. Infantry; taken prisoner at Pittsburg Landing and escaped. While on a train on the Columbus and Memphis railroad, he fell from the car and was killed, Sept. 21, 1868, in the 23d year of his age. His mother is now Mrs. Frederick Bates, of Stamford.

THOMAS R. GRAHAM, Co. B, 17th Conn., had been an apprentice to the printing business here, with Lieut. E. Hoyt. On Mr. Hoyt's enlistment, he returned from the city, where he was at work, and enlisted. He was killed in the engagement at Chancellorsville, May 2, 1863.

WILLIAM GILLESPIE was taken prisoner at Gettysburg, and died in the rebel prison of Belle Isle, leaving a family here.

BENJAMIN L. GREAVES, a native of Windham, Conn., was living in the family of the author when the war opened. Enlisting as private into Co. G, 10th Conn., he soon showed capacity for command, and was rapidly promoted to a captaincy. He was in thorough sympathy with the aim of the war, and in several engagements displayed the best qualities of a good captain. The summer of 1863 was especially trying to his health, and he was obliged to go into hospital on the first of October. For some thirty days, in the vicinity of Petersburg, Va., his company had been under fire, often, both day and night, and the exposure and strain proved too much for his nerves. He resigned, and was honorably discharged October 25, 1863.

Returning to New York City, where he had spent a large portion of his earlier life, he died there of congestion of the brain, August 10, 1868, leaving a wife to whom he had been married but a few months. His remains were taken to Windham, and deposited beside those of his father, in the beautiful cemetery of his native town.

The following testimony from Rev. H. C. Trumbull, chaplain of the Tenth, is worthy a place in our record of the captain's service : " Captain Greaves will ever be remembered by his army comrades, as a brave soldier, possessing fine qualities of mind, and many attractive traits of personal character. The fact that he was in command of the company, in the ranks of which he went out from Stamford, when hardly a year of his enlistment had expired, and that, too, in a regiment comprising such material as the Tenth, with its bright record for discipline, hard fighting and thorough efficiency evidenced his superiority in much that went to make a first-class soldier."

General J. L. Otis, in referring to captain Greaves' efficiency, while in command of a skirmish line at Deep Run, Va., Aug. 16, 1864, adds this estimate of his military character. " His conduct was always commendable in action. He was one of the kind not likely to get all the credit due to him. He never got excited under fire, and consequently did not make so much display to attract attention as others less deserving might. I always considered coolness and self-possession in action the most valuable characteristics an officer could possess, and captain Greaves had these in a remarkable degree."

At the annual reunion of the officers of the Tenth, Sept. 23, 1868, they thus testify to the military character of the captain :

" Captain Greaves, enlisting at the organization of the regiment, was soon promoted from the ranks for his gallantry and his faithfulness in duty. Step by step he won the command of a company, and thenceforward in prolonged and arduous army service, he ever bore himself as a brave, prompt and efficient soldier. Never flinching in the hour of danger, never failing in the performance of any task assigned him, he won the confidence of his commanders, and the respect of those whom he commanded. His record of patriotic services is one in which those who love him may have just pride, and his early death is sincerely lamented by many who knew his capabilities of usefulness."

GEORGE W. HARTSON, Co. B, 28th Conn., was wounded at Port Hudson, July 6, 1863, by a cap blown from one of our shells. He died from the wound and was buried at Port Hudson, August 1, 1863, leaving a wife and one daughter.

HORACE P. HOBBY, Co. D, 6th Conn., an excellent soldier and officer, one of the six sons of HARVEY HOBBY, of Stamford, who volunteered for the service, was captured near Bermuda Hundred, June 17, 1864, and with the others of his company captured with him, was taken to Richmond, and began his experience of prison life in Libby. He was removed to Andersonville, and successively endured the privations of Millen, Savannah, Charleston, and Florence, until the Thanksgiving morning of November, 1864, when he was taken up by two attendants and borne out from his prison to be sent to Annapolis for exchange—"the happiest thanksgiving," he said to his mother, on reaching home, December 29th, "that I ever knew." At home he lingered on in great suffering and weakness for nearly two years, yet never able to rally after the horrible sufferings of those wasting months,—more heroic even than on the battle field, where he had never flinched, until, a patient and brave martyr, he went to his rest and triumph, November 17, 1866, aged twenty-one years.

WILLIAM HOBBY, an older brother of Horace P., above, Co. F, 3d Conn., after returning from his three months campaign, returned to his business in town, and subsequently removed to Darien. On the 6th of March, 1868, as he was walking on the track of the railroad, a short distance from his house, he was suddenly struck and killed by an engine. He left a wife and three children.

JOSEPH HOLMES, Co. B, 29th Conn. died May 30, 1864.

ANDREW HOYT, son of Isaac Hoyt, of Stamford, Co. B, 28th Conn., after the trying summer of 1863, on the Mississippi, died soon after his regiment started homewards. His remains were interred on the Arkansas shore, just before sunset, Aug. 10, 1863.

EMMET M. HOYT, 3d Md., died probably at Little Washington, Va. He was an orphan at the opening of the war, son of Emmet, and grandson of Dea. Calvin Hoyt, with whom he was living. He was an amiable and excellent young man, with fine gifts of mind as well as heart.

JOHN E. HOYT, son of John, of Norwalk, Co. A, 28th Conn. died after four weeks sickness at Pensacola, Fla., Sunday, Feb 22, 1863. His remains were buried in the old Spanish cemetery in the center of Pensacola, with a soldier's head board to mark the grave. After the war they were disinterred and removed to the family lot in Norwalk.

SAMUEL B. HOYT, son of Benjamin Hoyt, Co. G, 10th Conn., after a brief service he found his lungs diseased and was discharged Oct. 21, 1861. He reached home and died Nov. 2d, of quick consumption, leaving a wife and four children.

SETH H. HOYT, son of Ezra Hoyt, Co. B, 28th Conn., was wounded at Port Hudson, June 14, 1863, and sent to the Baton Rouge Hospital on the 20th. He left a wife and two children.

HENRY W. HOYT, son of John M. Hoyt, Co. D., 6th Conn., for more than a year served as a faithful soldier. In the sharp engagement at Pocotaligo, Oct. 22, 1862, he was wounded by a grape shot which shattered his ankle badly. He had been one of the foremost in the fight, cheerful, courageous, and more thoughtful for others than himself. On receiving the wound which was to prove mortal, he was taken on to a litter and carried back from the front. Though in intense agony, as he passed his company with their faces still set against the enemy, his zeal for the cause for which he had been struck down overcame his agony, and with a hero's benediction in his looks of mortal paleness he left with them, also, the benediction of his prayer, " God be with you, boys." His limb was taken off, though too late to save his life. He was taken to Hilton Head. After lingering in great pain he died October 30th, and was buried in the lot selected for the soldiers' cemetery.

THOMAS S. INGERSOL, son of Alexander and Caroline Ingersol, was born in Stamford, Dec. 22, 1834. He entered the service of the Government in the war from a sense of duty, and never shrank from any hardship or exposure to which it called, until his health gave way and he was obliged to yield. At Roanoke he took a severe cold which settled upon his lungs from which he never recovered. He was greatly benefitted by the season spent in Florida with his company, and on returning Northward again into active service, unable to enter the ranks, he took the duty of teamster, in which service he remained to the close of the war. On returning home he found himself utterly broken down. His voice failed, and the disease which had been fastening itself on his lungs, at length triumphed. After a lingering illness, this exemplary citizen and good soldier made the last sacrifice he could make for his country, in the gift of his own life. He died at the homestead of the family, Oct. 24, 1866, and his remains lie in the family burying ground in the neighborhood of his home.

CHARLES JENNINGS, Co. B, 28th Conn., was in hospital at Memphis, from Aug. 13, 1863, and died leaving a wife and a daughter who soon died. His widow re-married and now lives in Norwalk.

EDWIN B. JESSUP, Co. B, 17th Conn., was taken with the typhoid fever at Brooks' Station, Va., of which he died, March 2, 1863. His funeral was attended in Stamford, March 21st, by Rev. Mr. Francis, and his remains interred in the Northfield burying lot.

BENJAMIN JONES, Co. H, 13th Conn., enlisted, Jan. 8, 1862, and died, April 8, 1862.

JOSEPH JONES, Co. D, 6th Conn., was slightly injured on Morris Island, and was mortally wounded before Petersburg where he died, June 9, 1864. He was a good soldier.

IRA D. JONES, Co. B, 6th Conn., was wounded at Fort Wagner, July 18, 1863, by a shot which entering the knee as it was bent, passed up into the femur, following the center of the bone about five inches, before its force was spent. It was found only after amputation of the limb. He lingered in great pain until his death, July 29th. His remains in the Fall following were brought to Stamford and deposited in the family lot at High Ridge. His father, Thaddeus Jones, has for several years lived in the Borough.

THERON B. JUNE, Co. G, 6th Conn., son of Wm. and Eliza June, entering the service near the close of the war commended himself by his fidelity and was appointed corporal, Dec. 19, 1864, even in a veteran corps. On Feb. 29, 1865, after chasing a rebel force through Wilmington, N. C., out to the N. E. Ferry, while at his evening meal, he was wounded by a shot from a sharpshooter. He was taken to the hospital in Baltimore, where he died, March 20, 1865, in the 18th year of his age.

Francis R. Leeds, Co. A, 10th Conn. See Stamford History, p. 401.

When his company left, early in Sept., 1862, to enter the Department of the Gulf, under Gen. Banks, Mr. Leeds was suffering from a typhoid fever, contracted during a previous visit to the South and West. As soon as he felt that his strength would bear it, he left to join his company. He reached them at Pensacola, Fla., on the 1st of Feb., 1863; and was soon struck down with a sudden and fatal attack of dysentery. His death occurred, Feb. 17, 1863. His remains were forwarded to Stamford, where they were interred in the new Woodland Cemetery. His funeral was attended from St. John's church, on Sunday, March 9th, when the sermon was preached by the Rector, Rev. Walter Mitchell. His testimony to the noble character of captain Leeds is full and explicit.

"When the young soldier went forth from us, it was in the full knowledge that he had taken his life in his hands, that he might be called upon at any moment to render it up. So far as it is permitted us to judge of human acts, it was not for himself that he went, it was no selfish ambition, but the holy conviction of duty under which he moved. And what more especially led him to the place so fatal to him, was his sense of responsibility to those who had trusted themselves to his guidance. Death, before failure of duty, was his choice. Others before self, responsibility before enjoyment, was the principle of his life."

Similar to this testimony was that of the Stamford *Advocate*, in its editorial notice of the funeral.

"It is long since this community has been visited by a loss so widely mourned. There was first to those entirely strangers to him the natural feeling of sorrow for one cut off in maintaining the great and holy cause of restoring the violated authority of the law. And when those came to learn from every lip, how gallant, how well-beloved and worthy of his post was the young commander, it would be with deepest regret that such an one should be taken when our country has so pressing a use for all her best and bravest.

"But the sympathy of strangers was nothing to the sorrow which has touched so very nearly the hearts of his many friends. More than any young man of his age and standing, captain Leeds had endeared himself to all classes of our citizens. In his business life as cashier of the Stamford Bank, his rare courtesy, his manliness, his tried integrity had won for him love and respect such as any one might court."

CHARLES W. LITCHFIELD, Co. A, 28th Conn. With considerable musical talent, he was a source of much entertainment for his comrades. After the war, he became partially deranged and died in Boston, Mass.

ANDREW J. LOCKWOOD, Co. A, 28th Conn., son of Sherman Lockwood, died from the fever of the locality, at Memphis, on the Mississippi, Sept. 19, 1863, leaving a family to mourn his untimely loss.

JAMES L. LOCKWOOD, brother of the above, Co. D, 6th Conn., saw much hard fighting, and incurred several serious risks. While on Morris Island, in one of the sharp engagements before Wagner, the plate of his belt was bent up, and he was sent rolling down a steep bank, without serious harm. In that engagement, near Bermuda Hundred, when his captain and so many of his comrades were captured he, also, was taken prisoner, and sent South. Death came to his relief at Andersonville, one of his comrades, Geo. E. Searles, being with him when he died.

SHERMAN D. LOCKWOOD, brother of the above, making three sons of Sherman Lockwood, who volunteered for the service, enlisted with his brother Andrew into Co. A, 28th Conn. Falling a prey to the fever of the Mississippi Valley, he was left at the hospital at Memphis, Aug. 13th, and died there, Sept. 9, 1863.

JOSEPH L. LOCKWOOD, 141st Penn. Infantry, a native of the town and son of the late Captain Edmund Lockwood, of Leroyville, Penn. His death occurred at Falmouth, Va., April 3, 1863, at twenty-four years of age. He is remembered here as an intelligent and sprightly youth and a worthy young man. His colonel paid him this high tribute: " His death is a most serious loss to his company and regiment. He was a most courteous gentleman and extremely active and efficient in the performance of his duty."

BANKS LOUNSBURY, Co. I, 2d Heavy Artillery, died Feb. 23, 1864, as the " Catalogue of the Connecticut Volunteer Force" testifies. He lived in Banksville, just off the extreme north-west corner of the town.

WILLIAM LOWA, Co. D, 6th Conn., was one of our first to fall in the desperate assault on Fort Wagner, July 18, 1863. He left a wife and children here. One of the children has been provided for at Fitch's Home in Darien.

HENRY LOWER, Co. A, 28th Conn., one of the three sons of Joseph Lower, who volunteered. He was sick in hospital at Baton Rouge, and is reported in the "Catalogue of the Connecticut Volunteer Force," as honorably discharged, Aug. 28, 1863. He was taken to New Orleans and put on board a transport with other invalid soldiers to be taken home, and has not since been heard from.

MURRAY MACREA, Co. B. 17th Conn., a ward of Thomas S. Hall, entered earnestly into the service and had a good record. With so many others of his company he was captured, May 19, 1864, and sent to Andersonville. On the approach of Sherman he was sent to Florence where he perished, a martyr to the Union cause, Jan. 1, 1865, but not before he had received a medal for meritorious service in the field.

HUGH MAHAN, Co. B, 17th Conn., was killed on the sharply contested field of Chancellorsville, May 2, 1863, leaving here a family.

JOHN H. MCDONALD, brother of Mrs. H. B. Lum, enlisted in the 82d N. Y. Volunteers for three months. He then re-enlisted for three years and was promoted orderly sergeant. He was wounded at Fair Oaks, May 31, 1862, and promoted 1st lieutenant for gallant service. He led his company in the fearful conflict of Gettysburg, and on the third day of the fighting, July 3, 1863, he fell on the battle field. His remains were afterwards brought to Stamford, and now lie in the Woodland Cemetery here. His brother Oliver was also in the service for more than three years, in one of the Pennsylvania regiments.

GEORGE A. MEAD, sergeant, Co. A, 28th Conn., had stood the nine months campaign, and returned to his family hoping soon to recruit his well nigh exhausted strength. Within a few days he was taken down with a malignant fever, and after a week's sickness, died, Sept. 6, 1863. He left a wife and a little daughter who did not long survive her father. His funeral was attended at St. John's by Rev. Mr. Mitchell and this son and excellent soldier of the town now lies beneath a monument placed over him by captain Wm. Skiddy.

HIBBARD MEAD, Co. H, 28th Conn., son of Reuben, died on the way home, at half past nine o'clock, A. M., Aug. 13, 1863, instead of the 10th, as the Adjutant's Catalogue reports it, and was buried the same day at Memphis.

CHAS. W. MILLER, a native of the town and son of Seth Miller. Though strongly attached to home, on the earnest call of the Government he enlisted into Co. B, 28th Conn. When the regiment left for home, after its nine months service, he was too feeble to accompany them, and he continued to decline until his death, Sept. 3, 1863, at Mound City. His remains were taken to Stamford, where they were interred, Sept. 6, 1863, from the Baptist church, of which he was a member. His memorial tablet is now on the walls of the Baptist Sunday School room, and his remains in the burying lot on Northfield street. He left a wife and four children to mourn his death, thus in the prime of his manhood. Their chief comfort was that he had nobly earned the title of Christian hero, and had gone to his triumph.

JOHN A. MILES, Co. D, 6th Conn. He was missed after the fighting of July 19, 1863, on Morris Island; and was afterwards reported in Andersonville; where he is supposed to have perished. He left a wife and two children. The children were in Fitch's Home in Darien, where the daughter died, Feb. 26, 1868.

WM. H. MONROE, Co. H, 1st Conn. Artillery, is reported as having died, May 16, 1864.

OBITUARY. 137

THOMAS W. MOLLET, Co. A, 28th Conn., son of John Mollet, of Stamford, and a young man of much promise. He was wounded at Port Hudson, and died in the Baton Rouge hopital, July 15, 1863.

WILLIAM A. MOREHOUSE, Co. D, 6th Conn., was a son of Mrs. John Bing by a former husband. He was killed at the assault on Fort Wagner, July 18, 1863.

CHARLES E. MORRELL, Co. B, 17th Conn., was son of Charles Morrell. He died at Beanfort, N. C., Oct. 3, 1863, in the thirty-first year of his age, leaving a wife and three children. The children have been provided for, a portion of the time since his death at Fitch's Home in Darien.

THEODORE NICHOLS, 6th N. Y. Cavalry, was son of Epenetus W. Nichols, and one of the four brothers furnished by that family for the war. He was shot by a sharpshooter, while pursuing with his regiment the fugitive Early up the Shenandoah.

SAMUEL S. OSBORN, Co. H, 17th Conn., son of Samuel. After re-enlisting in the 2d Heavy Artillery, he was wounded at the severe fighting of Cold Harbor, June 1, 1864. He was sent to Washington, D. C., and thence to McDougal hospital, Fort Schuyler, N. Y. When too late to save him, his right leg was amputated, after which he suddenly sank, and died June 30, 1864. His funeral was attended by Rev. L. W. Bacon at the Congregational church, July 3d, and his remains lie in the family lot in Woodland Cemetery. He left no family, his wife having died before his re-enlistment. He died at forty-five years of age, leaving the record of a good soldier. His last last words were those of a joyful christian, " I am almost home."

DAVID C. PALMER, Co. A, 6th Conn., son of James H.

Palmer, of North Salem, N. Y. On the breaking out of the war he had been living here about ten years. At Fort Wagner he was taken prisoner, and held as such in the prison at Columbia and Belle Isle. After being paroled he was taken on to Baltimore, where, being utterly exhausted, he died in the hospital, April 27, 1864. His remains were taken to Norwalk, the former residence of his wife, and interred in the family lot. His widow is still living in Stamford.

REUBEN PEATT, Co. G, 10th Conn., son of Reuben. After re-enlisting as veteran, he was sent to the hospital at Fortress Monroe, where he died.

WILLIAM L. PEATT, brother of Reuben, Co. D, 6th Conn. After his re-enlistment as veteran, he was shot through the body, May 16, 1864, at Bermuda Hundred, and never more heard from. The adjutant's report for 1865, gives his name as Pratt.

THEODORE H. PECK, son of Frederick Peck, Co. A, 28th Conn. During the campaign on the Mississippi river, he was taken down with fever. He was able to reach home, where he gradually declined until his death, Nov. 4, 1863, aged twenty-seven years. His funeral was attended from the Congregational church, of whose choir he had been a member. He had the rare gift of a heavy musical bass voice, and he used it often with happiest effects to relieve the tedium of camp life. It woke many a remembrance among his comrades of the dear old songs they had been wont to hear at home.

GABRIEL W. PLATT, son of John Platt, Co. A, 28th Conn. From N. W. Hoyt's Diary I learn that he was sent to the hospital at Port Hudson, Jan. 15, 1863, with dysentery, and died there on the 28th. His remains were interred in a ravine in the vicinity beneath "the tall magnolia trees of Port Hudson." He left a family of three children.

PATSY PICKER, son of Michael, Co. D, 6th Conn., died of fever, Oct. 5, 1863, at Hilton Head, where he was buried. He was only about seventeen years of age.

JOSEPH WILLARD POTTS, Co. B, 17th Conn., was killed at Chancellorsville, May 2, 1863.

JAMES A. POTTS, Co. D, 6th Conn., taken prisoner near Bermuda Hundred, and sent South with so many of his comrades to the severe doom of a rebel prison life. After his release, he was sent to Hilton Head where his exhausted strength gave out, and death came to his relief.

ALBERT M. POWELL, a native of Maryland; graduated at the U. S. Military Academy at West Point in 1860, and assigned to Co. H, 31st U. S. Inf. At the opening of the war he was promoted 1st Lieut. in the 13th U. S. Inf., and Capt. Oct. 24, 1861. He was transferred to the command of a battery in the 1st Missouri Volunteer artillery, and for meritorious service promoted lieutenant-colonel and chief of artillery in the 17th Army Corps. Here he "distinguished himself in several of the brilliant operations of the Western armies."

He married in Stamford, March 15, 1866, Julia, only daughter of N. E. Adams, Esq. He was soon ordered to Fort Stevenson, Dacota Territory, to defend our frontier against the Indians, to which post his wife accompanied him, remaining here until the spring of 1868, when, with her little one she left him, to spend the summer with her friends at the East. Soon the sad news followed of his sudden death. He had fallen from his horse, June 5, 1868, and received a fatal wound upon the head. He lingered, however, in an unconscious state until the 10th, when death released him. Of his death, Gen. R. de Trobriand, officially makes this report: "A serious loss to the army, and will be especially felt among his comrades and associates both in the volunteer and regular service, who could better appreciate his merits as an officer, and his refined qualities as a gentleman."

His remains were brought to Stamford and buried from the Congregational church, Aug. 23, 1868, in Woodland Cemetery. His widow and infant daughter are now residing here.

CHARLES E. PROVOST, Co. D, 6th Conn., was captured at Deep Run, and sent to Andersonville. After six months imprisonment he was released in a starving condition, and reached the hospital at Annapolis, Md., where three days later, death put an end to his sufferings. An excellent soldier.

CHARLES ROSBOROUGH, Co. A, 28th Conn., son of George and Honora Rosborough, was wounded at Port Hudson, June 14, 1863, by a ball which reached his heart, but without killing him. In attempting to escape from guerillas, while on his way to the hospital, at Baton Rouge, he was attacked by a sudden and fatal hemorrhage and died at the hospital July 11, 1863, at the age of twenty-four years. He left behind him the memory of a genial, generous-hearted young man, and his war record was that of a good soldier and a patriot citizen.

THEODORE C. SCOFIELD, Co. K, 6th Conn., died July 31, 1862.

WILLIAM ELLSWORTH SCOFIELD, son of Wm. Scofield, died in Memphis, Tenn., May 17, 1863, aged twenty-two years and three months. He had wished to enter the service while at home, but was dissuaded from doing so because of his physical inability. On a visit to his relations in Illinois, he could not resist the call made upon him, and entered the 74th Ill. regiment. He was for meritorious conduct, made orderly sergeant. He was a noble young man, and a courageous soldier. He was offered a discharge on account of his health, but refused to accept it. He continued to exhibit a model of fidelity in all the routine of a soldier's duty, until attacked by pneumonia, which proved suddenly fatal. A memorial service was held in his honor at the Congregational church of his native town, June 14, 1863.

GILBERT SCOFIELD, Co. A, 28th Conn., son of Seth Scofield, was taken with the fever while on the Mississippi, and was obliged to stop on the way home with the regiment, Aug. 18, 1863, at Cleveland, where he died on the 25th of the same month.

LEWIS B. SCOFIELD, Co. B, 28th Conn., son of James B. Scofield, was taken sick with fever at Brashear City, on the Mississippi, and sent to the hospital at New Orleans, where he died June 13, 1863, at thirty years of age. He was an excellent young man, and went into the service for the love he bore the Union, counting not his life dear to him, if he might serve so good a cause. His remains were brought home, and his funeral services were held in the Methodist church, attended by a large number of our people. The Rev. Dr. Sawyer, of New York, officiated, and his remains were deposited in the new Woodland Cemetery.

EDWARD M. SEELY, Co. D, 6th Conn., son of Thomas Seely, was wounded at Fort Wagner in 1863, and taken prisoner, Jan. 17, 1864, with so many of his comrades near Bermuda Hundred, and sent to Andersonville. After his release, while on the Baltic, he died before reaching Hilton Head, where he was buried.

BENJAMIN O. SEARLES, Co. B, 13th Conn., son of Edwin

G. and Maria O., went heartily into the service and made a good soldier. He was killed in the fiery charge at Irish Bend, April 14, 1863, in which "every soldier seemed eager to press forward to accomplish the object before him." He was one of the five sons furnished by this family for the service, and it was to his credit, that he stood well in one of the best regiments furnished by the State during the war.

GEORGE R. SEARLES, Co. A, 28th Conn., son of Ira Searles, was attacked on the Mississippi with the local fever and sent to the hospital at Mound City, where, after a sickness of about two weeks, as the faithful diary of Noah W. Hoyt testifies, he died Aug. 19, 1863.

GEORGE B. SELLECK, Co. B, 13th Conn., whose death, Sept. 29, 1862, is reported in the "Catalogue of the Conn. Vol. Force."

NATHAN SHERWOOD, Co. A, 28th Conn., son of Levi Sherwood, was another victim to the exposures of camp life on the Mississippi. He was left in hospital at Algiers, May 24th, according to N. W. Hoyt's diary, and died according to captain Charles Brown's report, July 30, 1863, at Port Hudson, where he was buried. He left a family here. He was in the twenty-eighth year of his age.

JOHN SIMMS, Co. G, 10th Conn. This excellent young man, when the war opened, was living with G. K. Riker, Esq., where he had won for himself a good name as a faithful and trustworthy young man. The testimonials which were given at his death are ample witnesses as to his excellent character. In the editorial which reports the funeral services we have this estimate of the departed soldier: "Early left an orphan, and with no near relative living, John Simms was a self-made man. He had none of the advantages which a finished education, or high social position gives, yet, by his manly deportment and strict integrity he had gained the esteem and good wishes of all who knew him."

The Rev. P. S. Evans, his pastor, in the funeral sermon which he preached Feb. 1, 1863, thus testifies:

"Our brother first became known to me in November, 1859, at which time he joined our church by letter. From the first he was loved and respected by all who knew him. * * * As a member of the church he was distinguished for manly earnestness and childlike humility. He was constant in his attendance. He labored with great self-distrust, but with scrupulous faithfulness in the Sabbath school. When, now nearly two years since, the echo of the guns of Sumpter sounded through the land, John Simms was one of those who stepped to the front. He said he had but one life, but that was at the service of his country. During that first three months of service none could have been more faithful as a soldier and a Christian than he. Every one spoke well of him. On his return he was asked if he had not seen enough of soldiering? 'No,' said he, 'the danger is more imminent now than then. My country calls more loudly than before. The horrible field of Bull Run was so disgraceful, both to officers and men, that it must be avenged.' After a brief respite he re-enlisted in the Tenth Conn. Here he won golden opinions from comrades and officers. He bore a gallant part in the battles of Roanoke Island and Newbern. Whoever may have flinched, he did not. He always spoke encouragingly and hopefully of the final issue."

Mr. Simms was sent home on recruiting service, and during his absence was promoted 2d lieutenant, when the Sunday School of the Baptist church presented him with a sword.

The occasion of his fatal wound, we have given us, in Mr. Evans' sermon. "An expedition was planned against

Kingston and Goldsboro, and the famous Tenth must share the dangers and the glory. He was not wanting at the post of danger, when it was the post of duty; and during the progress of the fight, at Kingston, Dec. 14, 1862, he received the wound of which he has since died. It was at first thought that the wound was slight. After lingering in uncertainty, mingled with hope and fear for three weeks, it became evident to all that he must die—and on the 11th of Jan., 1863, he fell asleep in Jesus." His remains now lie in our beautiful Woodland Cemetery.

Our hearts with their anguish are broken, our wet eyes are dim;
For us is the loss and the sorrow, the TRIUMPH for him.

PHŒBE CAREY.

SYLVANUS SMITH, Co. B, 28th Conn., like so many other of his comrades after the exposures on the Mississippi flats, during the summer of 1863, gave out on the way home, and was left in the hospital at Buffalo, where he died, Aug. 19, 1863, leaving here a wife and two children, of whom the wife and one child died soon after his death.

GROSVENOR STARR, adjutant, 7th Conn., son of Mrs. Henry B. Starr. See " Citizen Service," p. 29. Died at Tybee Island, March 5, 1862, after a sickness of five weeks. " Mr. Starr was at the breaking out of the war, a student at Yale. The idol of his classmates, who fondly watched his progress with warm anticipations of his future success, he was distinguished both for his scholarly attainments and his social qualities.

" There is no need of many added words to tell what he was. The one title, a christian soldier, covers all. At the age of fifteen, he girded himself with that heavenly armor, with which the soul encounters its unseen foes—the vows that he then renewed in confirmation. The emblems that were laid upon his coffin as it was borne by his sorrowing classmates to be laid before the altar, when were spoken the comforting words of the last service, were his completed epitaph. Above his breast rested the wreath of spotless flowers. Upon the hero's sword,—the gift of his loving classmates,—was placed the cross."

The funeral of Mr. Starr was attended from St. Bartholomew's church New York City, and his remains lie in the family lot in Greenwood.

ALBERT STEVENS, son of Albert Stevens of New Canaan, on the opening of the war, promptly volunteered for the service. He had already seen considerable service in the Florida war, and under Gen. Scott in Mexico. Having the reputation of an admirable tactician, and fired with an earnestly loyal zeal, he was commissioned captain of Co. F, 3d Conn. Volunteers. He served through the three months as captain of this company, winning in this service the reputation of one of our most courageous captains; and returning with the company was honorably discharged. He re-enlisted into the 17th Conn. and served in the ranks, but his health failing, he was detailed as hospital nurse. His death from disease occurred at Hilton Head, June 18, 1864. He left one son.

WM. T. STEVENS, Co. B, 17th Conn., was injured while felling trees for the encampment. He was sent to the hospital in Washington where he had a typhoid fever. He was afterwards sent to Fort Schuyler, where he obtained a pass to New York City for twenty-four hours to meet his wife. On his return he missed the boat and was therefore tardy in reporting. He was sent to the guard house where he took a cold, from which he never recovered. He died at Fort Schuyler, Feb. 4, 1863, leaving a wife to mourn over one of the most inconsolable hardships of a soldier's fate.

HENRY STOTTLAR, son of widow Catharine Stottlar, was born May 26, 1839. He enlisted into the Navy at the early age of fifteen, and served before the mast on the African coast. In 1862 he was on the U. S. Ship Onward, stationed at Savannah. With a boat's crew he was captured in July of that year, while on reconnoitering expedition and paroled. While on the voyage home, on the Ship Mountaineer, from Port Royal, on the 18th of April, 1863, he fell from the mizzen topsail yard, struck the rail, fell overboard and was drowned. One of his shipmates in a letter of condolence to the afflicted mother says of him: "he was loved on shipboard and honored on shore by all that knew him as an honest and upright young man." He was the youngest of the five sons of widow Stottlar, who volunteered into the service of the Government.

GEORGE C. SWATHEL, Co. D, 6th Conn., died Sept. 22, 1864.

He was a faithful soldier of whom his comrades thus testify, in their resolutions of condolence passed the day after his death. "We mourn him, now that he sleeps in a soldier's grave, as one in whom the service has lost a most devoted citizen soldier, his town and state a noble son, the cause another martyr, and his regiment an ornament."

Mr. Swathel left a wife and three children. By the timely provision of Benjamin Fitch, Esq., of Darien, his Orphans' Home had just been opened, and the two sons of the deceased soldier were well provided for, in their early orphanage. The widow and her daughter still reside in Stamford.

JOSEPH A. SUTTON, Co. H, 28th Conn., after being honorably discharged, July 28, 1863, with his regiment, was reported as having died.

JAMES LAWRENCE TAYLOR, 5th N. Y., Duryee's Zouaves, son of James and Jane E. Taylor, and born in New York

City, Sept. 7, 1840, was one of the earliest volunteers from the town. And he entered the service with all his heart, ready to dare and die if necessary. No importunity of his friends could dissuade him. His patriot plea for their consent was: "Could I be so craven as to prefer comfort with those I love, ease and luxury at home, while others are laying down their lives on the battlefield?" Though ill, on that fatal night when his company was ordered to prepare for the attack on Great Bethel, he was one of the first men ready for the march. And on the march of some twenty miles, he was buoyant and cheerful, with his never failing words of encouragement for his comrades, who were disposed to doubts and fears.

They approach the object of their march. Forewarned, the rebels are strongly entrenched behind their masked batteries. The forlorn charge is sounded and the desperate attempt fails. Early in the movement Taylor fell from a musket ball and was taken to the rear by his chaplain, Winslow, and Lieut.-Col. Warren, and provided for, in a family by the name of Dawson, about two miles from where he had fallen. There, after a night of suffering, with no word of complaint, yet, despite the mortal agony which was fast conquering his young life, with words of heroic cheer for the dear ones he had left behind, he breathed his last. "Tell them, I died on the battlefield, in a holy and glorious cause."

And so, the first representative from Stamford died, on the morning of June 11, 1861; and as its light dawned, they buried his remains in a field near the place of his last sufferings. His comrades, his colonel and his chaplain, agree in their affectionate testimonials to his excellent character, and to his admirable soldierly conduct. And no one can tell the loss which the stricken family felt when this dutiful son and loving brother, was so suddenly stricken down. But was it not honorable thus to die, on the same field, and in the same engagement in which Winthrop and Greble fell?

In June, 1865, his remains were recovered and now rest in the family lot at Greenwood.

JOHN J. TAYLOR, Co. B, 13th Conn., died at Thibodeaux, Feb. 17, 1864, leaving a family.

JOHN W. THORNE, Co. B, 13th Conn., is reported in the Catalogue of the Connecticut Volunteer Force, as dying, Sept. 6, 1863.

MARINUS W. THORNE, Co. D, 6th Conn., son of Lewis Thorne, was reported in the Catalogue of the Connecticut Volunteer Force, as deserting, Feb. 27, 1863. The report was made because he was not present at roll-call after his furlough had expired. He had left home to return, intending to join his company at New York, then on the way to the field again, but by some foul treatment, was disabled and robbed in New York. When the report of his desertion was made at Headquarters, he had already fallen a victim to the brutal treatment he had suffered. He died at one of the hospitals in New York, and his remains now lie among hundreds of his fallen comrades in the Cypress Hill Cemetery. His mother, now Mrs. G. S. Smith, is now living here.

WILLIAM H. TOTTEN, Co. A, 28th Conn., son of Hiram and Hannah Totten, died at Camp Ferris, Barrancas, Fla., March 28, 1863, of typhoid fever. His remains were buried in the Navy Yard cemetery on the following Sunday. He had been sick about three weeks, and was apparently recovering when the order was given to evacuate Pensacola. The removal to Barrancas was too much for him, the relapse which followed, proving fatal. "He was beloved by his company and all who knew him. He was always ready to do his duty, whatever it might be." Noble record for the young soldier, now dead. Every such record is an honor, not to the name alone of those who thus suffer and die, but to the family which has reared, and to the town which has lent such sons for such service.

JAMES VAIL, Co. A, 28th Conn., was killed in the assault on Port Hudson, June 14, 1863. He left a family.

GEORGE VANDERVALT, 1st Reserve Cavalry, Pa., was reported as shot through the head while in the service. He was one of the three sons of Soren Vandervalt, who were in the service.

JACOB W. VINCENT, Co. E, 17th Conn., son of Gilbert, was taken prisoner with so many of this company, May 19, 1864, in Florida, and sent into rebel prisons.

JAMES HENRY WALTERS, son of William and Delia (Hoyt) Walters, was born May 5, 1834. On the opening of the war, he offered himself as a volunteer to the Sixth Connecticut, but was rejected from physical disability. He went to New York and enlisted into Co. K, 14th N. Y. S. M., or the 84th N. Y. Volunteers. He was wounded, Aug. 2, 1862, and taken to the hospital at Washington, where he died, Aug. 2, 1862. He was a member of the Methodist church here, and left a wife and three children. Two of them, the children by a former wife, were taken to Fitch's Home in Darien, where one is still well cared for. His widow is yet living in Stamford.

WM. H. WALTON, Co. B, 28th Conn., son of Darius Walton, was another victim of the exposures of the Mississippi Valley. He died in the New Orleans Barracks Hospital, June 16, 1863, leaving here a family. Two of his children have found timely care and instruction in Fitch's Home in Darien.

JASON WARDELL, Co. A, 28th Conn., son of Henry and Lois Wardell. He was one of the three representatives of the town, who were killed in the unsuccessful assault made on Port Hudson, June 14, 1863. He was only twenty-two years of age, when he thus laid himself, a victim on the altar of his zeal for the cause which he served.

ANDREW C. WATERBURY, Co. A, 28th Conn., son of the late Webster Waterbury, of New York City. An amiable young man and a good soldier, was taken with the measles while in camp at Port Hudson. From a relapse, occasioned by drinking freely of spring water, he died Aug. 2, 1863, at twenty-two years of age.

STEPHEN R. WATERBURY, brother of the above, in the same company, and held in like esteem by his comrades, died Aug. 4, 1863, of the same disease with his brother, and from a similar relapse. Both of them were buried at Port Hudson where they died.

JOHN WATERS, Co. C, 28th Conn., son of Stephen Waters, died Aug. 1, 1863, leaving a family. One of his children has been provided for at Fitch's Home, in Darien. He is reported on the State "Catalogue of the Volunteer Force," as being honorably discharged Aug. 28, 1863, nearly a month after his death.

JAMES W. WEBB, son of Noah and R. E. Webb, born in Feb. 1846, and though only sixteen years old, enlisted April 10, 1862, into Co. A, 1st Conn. Artillery. He was noticeably a prompt and valiant youth and a good soldier. He shrunk from no exposure or hardship which was in the way of duty, and earned the confidence and good will of all his comrades in the service. He died Aug. 8, 1862, from fever, near Harrison Landing, on the James river, in Virginia. The body, embalmed, was forwarded to Stamford, and at the request which, in his thoughtfulness, he had made before leaving home, his funeral was attended from the Universalist church. His remains were the first which had been brought back to the town, and were deposited in the receiving tomb of the new Woodland Cemetery, until a lot should be purchased for the fallen soldiers of the town.

WILLIAM O. WEBB, Co. A, 28th Conn., son of Frederick Webb, was wounded June 14, 1863, at Port Hudson, and was sent to the hospital at Baton Rouge, where he died, June 30, 1863. His remains were buried there. He left a family.

GEORGE W. WILMOT, Co. C, 28th Conn., son of Theodore Wilmot. The third day after the assault on Port Hudson, June 17, 1863, as he was going out from his rifle pit to get a drink of water, he was shot through the heart. His remains were buried at Port Hudson.

WILLIAM E. WHITE, captain Co. K, 90th N. Y. S. M., a step son of the late Peter Smith, Esq., of Stamford. The following testimonial in the official notice of his death, is worthy a place on our record. It is addressed to Adjutant-General L. Thomas, U. S. Army, Washington, D. C., by Col. William Chapman, commanding the draft rendezvous, Wisconsin:

"It is with deep regret that I announce to you the death of Capt. William E. White, 90th New York Volunteer Infantry, Assistant Quartermaster at this rendezvous. He expired at 10.30 o'clock, A. M., Feb. 4, 1865, at his boarding house in the city of Madison, to which place he was removed from camp Randall, a few days previous to his death. Capt. White reported for duty, Nov. 30, 1864, and was appointed Acting Assistant Quartermaster on the 30th of that month, and although his constitution was much debilitated by disease, the result of exposure in the field, he discharged his duties in a most faithful and satisfactory manner, until within a few days of his death.

"Capt. White was highly esteemed and respected for his mild and agreeable manners, the general excellence of his character, and his devotion to the service in which he had volunteered." The remains of Capt. White were brought to Stamford. His funeral was attended in St. John's Church, Feb. 10, 1865.

GEORGE A. YOUNGS, Co. K, 8th New York artillery, died in Calver Hospital, Washington, D. C., from disease contracted in the service. His funeral was attended here, Oct. 12, 1864, in the Baptist Church. He was a young man held in high esteem, both for his intelligence and for his excellent social qualities.

FAMILIES REPRESENTED BY TWO OR MORE SONS.

On page 34 of our Citizen Service will be found a paragraph giving the number of our families which were represented in the service by three sons or more. It seemed desirable to indicate these families and the sons thus representing them. I have therefore completed and enlarged the list, as far as my means of information has allowed, and have also added to that list, those families which have furnished two sons for the service.

The family spoken of on page 34, as furnishing one son and seven grandsons is that of widow Alexander Ingersoll. Her grandsons were not all living in Stamford, though they so worthily represented the Stamford family.

The following is the list of these families, all of whose sons are heretofore reported on our military or naval record:

HARVEY HOBBY: Charles A., Theodore, Selah R., William, Horace P. and Albert.

WIDOW CATHARINE STOTTLAR; John, Jacob, Martin, Christopher and Henry.

LEWIS SCOFIELD: James T., Geo. A., Alfred V., Lewis W. and Noah T.

EDWIN G. SEARLES: John H., George E., Benjamin O., Henry C. and Clarence E.

E. WEBB NICHOLS: Charles H., James H., Theodore and and Edward F.

154 STAMFORD SOLDIERS' MEMORIAL.

William Walters: James H., Charles C., Edward H. and John W.
Michael O'Neil: Peter, William, Michael and Henry.
John Feeks: Joseph, Geo. D., William N. and Wright H.
Joseph Nichols: Nicholas N., John Q., Joseph and Nathaniel H.

Sherman Lockwood: A. J., S. D., and James L.
Deacon A. Scofield: Walter K., George A. and John O.
J. M. Hoyt: Henry W., Noah W., and John L.
Joseph Lower: Lewis, Henry and John.
Mrs. Mary A. Bing: William A. Morehouse, E. J. and Charles Bing.
Joseph Bouton: Theodore W., William H., and Spencer.
Webster Waterbury: Andrew C., Stephen R., and James W.
George W. Anderson: Joel M., Geo W., and Henry H.
Lewis Raymond: Cyrus J., Stiles and Bradford.
Seth Miller: Charles W., Theodore and John W.
Ezra R. Saunders: George F., Benjamin R. and W. W.
John Billings: Aaron, Isaac and Adam F.
Mrs. George W. Toms: Theodore W. Swan, Alonzo P. and George W. Toms.
Soren Vandervalt: George, Emanuel and John.
Deacon T. Davenport: Theodore, John and James B.
John Ferguson: John D., Samuel and Walter.

Calvin Chamberlain: Allen and George W.
Benjamin J. Daskam: James W. and Eugene B.
Hon. J. B. Ferris: Samuel P. and Isidore.
Thomas Gardner: Horace and Lewis.
Edwin Hoyt: George and John.
Isaac Hoyt: Andrew and George.
Aaron June: George W. and William H.

DANIEL JONES: Lewis and Nahor.
STEPHEN LOUNSBURY: Henry J. and S. R.
AARON MEEKER: Lorenzo and William H.
LEWIS McDONALD: Lewis and Robert.
GEORGE PROVOST: Andus and Charles E.
REUBEN PEATT: William S. and R. C.
WILLIAM PARKER: John and William.
SEYMOUR SEARLES: Edward and John E.
JAMES B. SCOFIELD: Geo E. and Lewis B.
H. K. SKELDING: H. T. and Thomas.
ISAAC SMITH: Charles W. and Stephen.
GEORGE W. SMITH: George G. and T. F.
SKINNER TOMS: Edgar and George.
DAVID WILMOT: H. L. and Joseph.
NOAH WEBB: Allen and James W.
JAMES WARREN: James and Joseph.
WILLIAM YOUNGS: George W. and John R.
ISAAC JONES: Cyrus D. and Isaac S.
ALEXANDER PROVOST: Chauncey and Norman.
R. W. SHUFELDT and R. W. Shufeldt, Jr.
JOHN R. YOUNGS and son Edward Youngs.

INDEX.

Abbot, Edward M................57
Ackley, Abram C...........91, 120
Adams, George.................89
Adams, Wm. D..................111
Allis, Wells............15, 42, 44
Anderson, Geo W...........54, 154
Anderson, Joel M..........54, 154
Anderson, Henry H....92, 111, 154
Arents, Edward................54
Arnold, A C...................64
Armstrong, Richard............88
Asia, Charles E...............93
Avery, A. S...................91
Avery, F. B...............91, 120
Ayres, Elbert..............7, 69
Ayres, Jas. R............100, 120
Ayres, S. L. P............54, 111

Badger, Geo. E...............101
Bailey, E. P..................85
Bailey, C. A..................44
Bailey, T. I........35, 44, 88, 120
Bailey, Wm. A.................81
Baker, Patrick...........94, 111
Ballard, Ela..............44, 85
Banks, Wm. H..................85
Banks, Allen..................93
Banks, Wm.....................93
Barber, James.................65
Barret, Isaac.........77, 79, 83
Barmore, Nath'l jr....35, 85, 120
Bates, Frederick..............54
Beardsley, Edson E.........44, 69
Bedient, Theodore.............94
Bell, Martin..................91
Bell, Charles.................85
Benedict, Geo.................92
Bennet, N. B........25, 77, 81, 86
Beresford, Henry..............90

Betts, Charles E..............98
Billings, Aaron...........83, 154
Billings, Isaac...........83, 154
Billings, Adam F..........83, 154
Bing, Ed. J., jr.....44, 54, 120, 154
Bing, Charles................154
Birdsell, S. S................94
Bishop, Hanford..............100
Bishop, J. E..................95
Bishop, Alfred................65
Bishop, Wm. H.................95
Bishop, Fred.................100
Blake, Benj. G................65
Bodey, S. I...................82
Bohan, John..........54, 65, 121
Botts, John H.................53
Bouton, Seth S................54
Bouton, James E...............98
Bouton, John E...........83, 121
Bouton, Wm. C.................83
Bouton, Theodore W.......83, 154
Bouton, Wm H.............83, 154
Bouton, Spencer......83, 121, 154
Bouton, Saml. M...............85
Bouton, Ezra C........35, 95, 121
Boyd, Andrew..........35, 85, 121
Brantingham, Chas. N.........112
Brady, A. G.......7, 21, 22, 23, 68
Brewer, Wm H..................94
Brodhurst, A Z................73
Brown, Smith..................44
Brown, George.................57
Brown, Wm.....................57
Brown, Chas. H..7, 21, 74, 75, 77, 80, 81
Brown, Chas. J................83
Brown, John..............93, 122
Brown, George E...............93
Brown, Seeley.................83

Brown, Chas. H.................107
Brown, Chas. W................107
Brown, Phineas............88, 122
Brown, Thomas L...............92
Brown, Wm. H..................93
Bryson, Frank.........35, 54, 122
Burke, Michael................93
Burns, Dennis..............54, 69
Bunten, Robert................82
Bunten, G. R..................86
Bush, Harry...................57
Butcher, John.................86
Buttry, John..............69, 122
Buttry, John D................73
Buxton, Jas. N................82
Brush, John H................107

Cahill, Timothy...............90
Cash, Martin..................69
Card, B. W....................85
Card, Wm. H...................89
Carey, Giles..................53
Caldwell, Samuel..........86, 122
Caldwell, C. W................86
Capper, Henry M.........7, 44, 64
Carrigan, M...................95
Carrol, John.................100
Carrol, Morris.........64, 94, 123
Canfield, J. H................94
Cavenough, Peter.............112
Chadwick, John H..............69
Christison, G. B..............69
Chamberlain, G. W....70, 103, 154
Chamberlain, Allen...98, 112, 154
Chaney, Wm....................90
Clark, J. S...............54, 123
Clark, John...................55
Clark, E. T...............86, 123
Clock, Geo. W.............83, 123
Cline, John H.................93
Conlan, James.............44, 89
Conley, C. H..................85
Coyne, Wm. H..................55
Corris, Joseph................65
Collins, James................90
Collins, John.................70
Collins, Michael..............89
Cook, L. A................89, 123
Connelly, John................90
Conklin, F. W.................94
Conklin, J. L.................94
Conner, Jeremiah..............95

Conner, Daniel................95
Conroy, Peter................112
Comstock, David C., jr....7, 73, 102
Councel, Charles..............90
Crocker, Albert W.............55
Craw, Thomas..................55
Crague, J. M..................65
Crabb, E. S...................70
Crabb, George.................83
Crabb, George R...............83
Crabb, W. H...................86
Crissey, Andrew...........86, 124
Cunningham, J. R...........57, 83
Curtis, Hiram................107
Daily, F. R...............99, 124
Dann, Smith...................83
Daskam, E. B......79, 80, 82, 154
Daskam, Jas. W............97, 154
Daskam, John W............58, 124
Dayton, C. I..............44, 112
Davenport, Jas. B........108, 154
Davenport, John..24, 102, 107, 154
Davenport, Theodore, jr..107, 154
Deiner, Carl..................57
Decker, David................112
Decker, Peter................112
Delemater, James.............112
Dever, Cornelius.............112
Dever, Richard...............112
Dever, Cornelius..............88
Deleroix, Theodore...14, 15, 44, 88
Dixon, Alonzo.................55
Dixon, Clark..................91
Dixon, Levi...................73
Dixon, S. S...............77, 83
Dinger, Isaac.................57
Dillon, Daniel...............113
Dillon, Richard..............113
Drew, David R................113
Drew, John....................55
Drewer, Charles...............57
Dunham, Wm....................69
Durand, Charles.......78, 85, 124
Ebbets, Geo. A...............113
Egan, Michael.................70
Ensley, O. S..................86
Eldridge, Geo. A..............85
Ellis, Joseph.................93
Essex, Wm.....................92
Evans, P. S. 7, 14, 16, 18, 19, 23, 26, 98

INDEX.   159

Farrel, James 90
Farrel, John 70
Farrel, Patrick 103
Farnold, Wm 70, 124
Farrington, A. E 83
Fagan, Wm 94
Ferris, Ed. A 44, 83
Ferris, D. W 57
Ferris, W. I 91, 125
Ferris, Wm. H 65
Ferris, Jas. N 83
Ferris, A. P 86
Ferris, B. P 86
Ferris, Isaac 86
Ferris, Isidore 113, 154
Ferris, Saml. P., 73, 74, 76, 81, 103, 154
Ferguson, John D 107, 154
Ferguson, Samuel 107, 154
Ferguson, Walton 108, 154
Feeks, Joseph 70, 153
Feeks, Geo. D 70, 125, 153
Feeks, Wm. N 153
Feeks, Wright H 88, 153
Fessenden, Saml 100
Fermin, Joseph 92
Finch, Geo. W 91
Finch, David 55
Finch, Charles E 55
Finch, Geo W 53
Fish, G. W 99
Fitzpatrick, Patrick 70
Fitzpatrick, John 70
Foster, J. G 86
Fox, Patrick 57, 125
Fox, Michael 35, 70, 125
Fox, Thomas 113
Freeman, Daniel 55, 125
French, B. F 113
Francis, Rev. E 32, 99
Fryermuth, P 35, 86, 125
Fuller, P. C 104, 126

Gay, Eugene 57
Ganung, Stephen 57
Gagan, John 86, 113
Gardiner, Horace 98, 154
Gardiner, Lewis 98, 154
Gardner, Lewis 113
Gardner, Joseph 113
*Gaylor, C. H 113

Gilmore, J. D 44
Gillespie, Wm 35, 70, 126
Gilbert, J. M 83
Gibson, Joseph 99
Gibson, Joseph 2d 113
Giblin, James H 113
Glendining, Geo. W 113
Grady, John 55
Greaves, B. L ... 7, 59, 60, 61, 62, 126
Graham, Thomas R 70, 126
Green, Simon 93
Gray, Stephen 92
Gifford, E. S 109

Hayward, F 77, 83
Hartson, G. W 35, 86, 126
Hartman, John 70
Harrison, E. O 69
Halpin, Wm 57, 88
Hawkins, W. H 93
Hannagan, M 99
Hannagan, Edward 108
Hanford, George 57
Hanford, John 100
Hallock, F. Wm 98
Halleck, T. M 113
Hall, Samuel T 70
Hall, Wm. L 86
Hawley, F. M 22, 113
Harris, Thomas S 91
Harvey, John 44, 67, 69
Hassenan, John F 55
Haight, John J 90, 57
Hays, Wm. L 65
Hendricks, W 95
Henry, James 94
Heiser, George 70
Heiser, Martin 70
Hennesey, Patrick 70
Hicks, Harrison 84
Hobby, Charles A. 23, 42, 67, 68, 153
Hobby, Theodore 113, 153
Hobby, Horace P ... 49, 53, 128, 153
Hobby, William 44, 128, 153
Hobby, Selah R 69, 153
Hobby, Albert 113, 153
Holly, A. J 83
Holly, J. M 113
Holly, H. S 86
Holly, Henry H 97
Holly, Pierre R 101
Holly, Francis M 103

*Misprinted Taylor.

Holly, Charles H. 107
Holmes, Charles P. 107
Holmes, Joseph. 129
Holmes, Samuel H. 107
Holton, John A. 89
Hood, Joseph 93
Hoovey, Joseph. 57
Howell, H. J. 83
Hounslow, Roper. 48, 55
Hounslow, Eli. 70
Hoyt, George. 73, 154
Hoyt, John 98, 154
Hoyt, J. E. 83, 129
Hoyt, I. F. 86
Hoyt, S. H. 35, 86, 129
Hoyt, Samuel B. 64, 129
Hoyt, Lyman. 86
Hoyt, Emmet M. 101, 129
Hoyt, Andrew 35, 86, 129, 154
Hoyt, George. 55, 154
Hoyt, H. W. 55, 130, 154
Hoyt, Noah W. 83, 154
Hoyt, John L. 55, 103, 154
Hoyt, Edgar. 7, 68
Hoyt, Joseph N. 70
Hoyt, Lorenzo L. 35, 71
Hoyt, Frank 107
Hoyt, Oliver. 107
Hoyt, Samuel B. 107
Hoyt, Charles W. 107
Hudson, George. 113
Hurd, Peter. 101
Hunter, John. 57
Hull, John. 58
Husted, Alfred N. 64
Hurlbutt, Lewis R. 107

Inness, W. H. 54
Ingersoll, T. S. 64, 130
Ingersoll, Samuel C. 101
Ingersoll, Alva. 99
Irving, Thomas 90

Jackson, Henry R. 86
Jackson, Henry. 58
Jackson, W. H. 71
Jennings, Charles. 35, 87, 131
Jerman, James H. 55
Jessup, John D. 84
Jessup, E. B. 69, 131
Jimmerson, H. F. 77, 84
Jones, Andrew T. 63

Jones, Francis H. 88
Jones, Benjamin. 91, 131
Jones, William P. 7, 14, 19, 103
Jones, I. D. 54, 131
Jones, James. 55
Jones, Joseph. 55, 131
Jones, B. H. 91
Jones, C. D., 24, 25, 26, 76, 80, 85, 107, 155
Jones, Isaac S. 107, 155
Jones, Lewis. 85, 154
Jones, Nahor. 86, 154
Jones, Alva. 86
Jones, F. A. 100
Johnson, David. 93
Johnson, William. 90
Johnson, Samuel H. 113
June, Jacob. 94
June, John L. 71
June, William H. 86, 154
June, G. W. 87, 154
June, Theron B. 58, 131
June, Elbert. 107

Kane, Martin. 114
Kapf, Frederick. 58
Keeler, Philip B. 83
Keeler, Smith O. 64
Keegan, James. 101
Keller, William. 89
Kelly, John. 44
Kelly, John 2d. 44, 71
Kelly, Patrick 95
Kennedy, Daniel. 71, 114
Kennedy, Dennis. 114
Kent, George W. 55
Kennaday, Edward. 108
Ketcham John. 114
Kirk, Warren. 73
King, William H. 85
Kiley, John. 114
Knapp, R. S. 64
Knapp, James K. 91
Knapp, Theodore. 84
Knapp, Charles W. 7, 87
Knapp, C. W. 96
Kreig, Jacob. 14, 71
Kreig, C. H. 44
Krollpheifler, F. 98

Lapham, H. H. 114
Lattan, Abram. 93

INDEX. 161

Lasher, Oscar................98
Lawrence, Zophar............114
Lawrence, E. B...............85
Lawler, John.................58
Lawler, Thomas...............89
Leonard, John...............114
Lee, Henry..................114
Leeds, F. R......23, 24, 26, 81, 132
Lever, Philip.......24, 44, 80, 82
Leeds, Edward F.............107
Lind, James..................94
Lilley, John.............89, 91
Lincoln, George W............71
Litchfield, Charles W......84, 132
Lloyd, George...............114
Lower, Lewis.............55, 154
Lower, Henry........84, 134, 154
Lower, John.......77, 79, 84, 154
Lowe, Frederick..............87
Lowa, William............54, 134
Lounsbury, H. L......44, 69, 155
Lounsbury, S. R...........64, 155
Lounsbury, Banks........94, 134
Lord, George.................54
Lowney, Thomas...............87
Lockwood, George E...........64
Lockwood, Charles H..........54
Lockwood, A. L..............114
Lockwood, Samuel 2d..........87
Lockwood, Charles M..........55
Lockwood, E. C...............91
Lockwood, E. A...............91
Lockwood, A. J......55, 84, 134, 154
Lockwood, S. D...35, 84, 134, 154
Lockwood, James L.....55, 133, 154
Lockwood, Samuel R...........87
Lockwood, William H..........87
Lockwood, George.............98
Lockwood, Joseph S......101, 134
Lum, William B..............114
Lynott, James................64
Loescheyk, Otto.............117

Macrea, Murrey H.........69, 135
Manahan, M..................114
Manning, John...............104
Mahon, Hugh.........35, 75, 135
Marlin, Richard..............71
McDonald, J. H...........99, 135
McDonald, William............98
McDonald, Lewis..........71, 155
McDonald, Robert.........55, 155

McCarty, James..............100
McClellan, J. A..............95
McCormick, A.................94
McGee, James.................54
McQueen, Frank...............90
McKeon, Patrick.............114
Mead, George A...35, 77, 79, 82, 135
Mead, Hanford................77, 84
Mead, Hibbard............89, 136
Meeker, William H........53, 155
Meeker, Lorenzo 7, 11, 14, 16, 46, 50, 52, 155.
Meeker, George H.........71, 88
Mitchell, Robert.............92
Miller, Anthony..............96
Miller, A. E................114
Miller, Theodore..44, 45, 44, 63, 99, 154
Miller, Charles W...35, 87, 136, 154
Miller, John W...........96, 154
Miller, C. E.................88
Miller, R. S................108
Minor, John C...............102
Minor, William T.....19, 21, 22
Miles, John A.......35, 55, 130
Moor, Richard................96
Morgan, Michael..............55
Morgan, Alonzo S.............82
Morehouse, W. A....56, 137, 154
Moram, James.................58
Morris, James................58
Morrison, S. C...............73
Meyer, Aaron J...............65
Morrell, C. E......35, 71, 137
Mollett, T. W............84, 137
Monroe, William H........94, 136
Mulholland, J................94
Myers, Richard...............92
Murphy, Michael..............44

Newman, Charles..............58
Newman, J. M................114
Newell, John B...............65
Nellis, William..............92
Nichols, Watson B............96
Nichols, N. N............64, 154
Nichols, Joseph..........64, 154
Nichols, N. H............88, 154
Nichols, Charles H...50, 51, 52, 153
Nichols, John Q..........64, 154
Nichols, James H.........85, 153
Nichols, Theodore....97, 137, 153

STAMFORD SOLDIERS' MEMORIAL.

Nichols, Edward F......44, 114, 153
Northrop, Silas.................56
Northrop, Corvus..............90
Nodyne, Thomas...............87
Norman, Ebenezer..............90
Nolan, William................98
Nugent, E. G..................64

Oakes, William C..............58
O'Brien, Thomas............35, 89
O'Brien Frank.................56
O'Brien, John.................94
Oldrin, Edward................99
O'Neil, Michael............96, 154
O'Neil, Peter.............96, 154
*O'Neil, William........114, 154
O'Neil Henry;.............104, 154
O'Reily, Jeremiah.............93
Osborn, S. S..........73, 94, 137
Olmstead, James H............107

Paight, Joseph........44, 78, 88
Packet, Henry.................96
Palmer, David C..........58, 137
Palmer, C. H..................99
Palmer, E. E..................87
Palmer Nathan.................90
Parker, A. L..................84
Parker, John..............98, 155
Parker, William...........98, 155
Parks, Rev. J. H.............102
Parketon, Lewis...............71
Payne, E. T...................92
Peatt, William S..........56, 138
Peatt, Reuben.............65, 138
Peck, T. H................84, 138
Peck, Alonzo..................95
Pender, J. W..................58
Pember, Joseph L..............92
Phyfe, S. M...................99
Potts, James A...........56, 139
Potts, Joseph W..........71, 139
Potts, George H...............94
Poinsett, P...................90
Powell, Albert M........104, 139
Powell, William...............98
Picker, Patsey...........56, 139
Picker, Thomas................56
Pinkham, J. D.................94
Pierson, Richard.............101
Platt, G. W..........35, 82, 138

*Misprinted Henry.

Pratt, G. H...................90
Pratt, Edgar L................56
Provost, Norman........49, 53, 155
Provost, Chauncey.........108, 155
Provost, Chas. E......54, 140, 155
Provost, Andrus...........56, 155
Provost, Lewis................84

Quigley, E. H.................71
Quintard, E. A................99

Rairden, P....................94
Rankin, Peter................114
Randall, Daniel...............87
Rambo, S. S...................65
Rafferty, J...................84
Raymond, Bradford........99, 154
Raymond, Cyrus J........84, 154
Raymond, Stiles......77, 82, 154
Reynolds, W. H................54
Repke, John...................71
Riley, John T................102
Rooney, Peter.............15, 45
Rockwell, Henry..........81, 104
Rosborough, C. A....77, 79, 84, 140
Roscoe, Henry H...............87
Romer, William H..............97
Rowan, J. H..................114
Rusher, C. J..................87
Raeburn, Alexander...........108
Rosborough, John.............108

Saunders, B. R...........100, 154
Saunders, W. W.......77, 87, 154
Saunders, Geo. E.........87, 154
Scofield, James T.....45, 72, 153
Scofield, Geo. A......45, 69, 153
Scofield, Alfred V........69, 153
Scofield, Lewis W........69, 153
Scofield, Noah T.........87, 153
Scofield, W. K..........115, 154
Scofield, Geo. A.......114, 154
Scofield, John O........111, 154
Scofield, George E.......87, 155
Scofield, Lewis B....87, 144, 155
Scofield, T C............58, 140
Scofield, Henry...............56
Scofield, Smith...........56, 77
Scofield, D. C................85
Scofield, S. S................87
Scofield, D. H............44, 97
Scofield, Wm..................87

INDEX.   163

Scofield, J. E..................87
Scofield, Saml................72
Scofield, A. P.................88
Scofield, Charles.............98
Scofield, Chs. M.............108
Scofield, Wm. E........101, 140
Scofield, James..............104
Scofield, Leroy...............108
Scofield, Saml................72
Scofield, Gilbert..........84, 141
Scofield, A. W................82
Scofield, Geo. E..............84
Scofield, S. L.................84
Scofield, Andrew..............84
Scofield, Smith...............84
Scofield, Loomis..............84
Scofield, Wm. H...............72
Scofield, Robert B...........107
Scriber, Thomas...........47, 54
Searles, John H..........100, 153
Searles, Geo. E............56, 153
Searles, Benj. O......91, 141, 153
Searles, Henry C......91, 100, 153
Searles, Clarence E.......58, 153
Searles, Edward...........56, 155
Searles, John Ennis.......91, 155
Searles, Geo. R...........84, 142
Searles, Geo H................91
Searles, Mortimer.............72
Seaman, Albert...............96
Seely, E. M................56, 141
Selleck, Hobby...............115
Selleck, George B.........91, 142
Selleck, Benjamin.............94
Selleck, A. S...............77, 84
Sherwood, Henry A.............84
Sherwood, Nathan.........84, 142
Sherwood, Aaron J.............65
Sherwood, John................65
Shower, Fred..............99, 115
Shufeldt, R. W............115, 155
Shufeldt, R. W., jr.......115, 155
Simms, John....26, 45, 61, 63, 143
Simpson, Peter................90
Skiddy, Wm. W...............107
Skelding, H. T...........115, 155
Skelding, Thomas..........96, 155
Slater, John..................87
Sloan, W. M..................104
Smalart, John.................72
Smith, G. G...............58, 155
Smith, T. F...............58, 155

Smith, Chas. L................87
Smith, Sylvanus...35, 65, 87, 144
Smith, Edwin L................72
Smith, S. S...................82
Smith, Stephen............84, 155
Smith, Chas. W............96, 155
Smith, John H.................93
Smith, Wm. W.................97
Smith, Edwin L...............104
Smith, Henry V................95
Smith, Chas. J...............108
Smith, James.................107
Sniffin, Irving L..............56
Sniffin, James...............115
Snively, David................93
Snyder, O. E..................56
Sparks, John S................56
Stanley, Thomas...............87
Steinert, Henry..............115
Steinert, George..............72
Staples, S. C................102
Starr, Henry..................93
Starr, Eli....................94
Starr, Grosvenor..........89, 144
Stevens, Albert...40, 43, 44, 72, 145
Stevens, Alonzo..............108
Stevens, Clark...............115
Stevens, M. J.................88
Stevens, Hennel..............102
Stevens, Wm. T...........72, 145
Stevens, Wm. H................88
Stevens, Chauncey.............95
Still, F. L.........45, 58, 104
Stottlar, John...48, 49, 51, 53, 153
Stottlar, Jacob...........52, 153
Stottlar, Martin....47, 49, 53, 153
Stottlar, Christopher......69, 153
Stottlar, Henry......115, 146, 153
Stockton, J. W................73
Strant, J. R..................95
Stark, Andrew................107
St. John, John...............107
Sutton, Joseph A..........89, 146
Sullivan, John................99
Swan, Theodore W.........45, 154
Swathel, George C....35, 56, 146
Swertcope, J. V.......77, 79, 84
Swartwout, Robert............107
Swartwout, Satterlee.........107

Tanner, Abel..................85
Taylor, Nehemiah..............58

Taylor, Chas. H. 113	Wardell, J. 77, 78, 85, 150
Taylor, George W. 90	Warner, F. R. 76, 81, 82, 98
Taylor, John J. 35, 91, 148	Warren, Geo. L. 107
Taylor, Wm. S. 84	Warren, James C. 99, 155
Taylor, Wm. 85	Warren, Joseph R. 97, 155
Taylor, James L. 96, 146	Waterbury, C. W. 88
Thorne, M. W. 56, 148	Waterbury, Philip. 88
Thorne, John W. 91, 148	Waterbury, Geo. P. 107
Thompson, Chas. E. 108	Waterbury, Marcus. 23, 44, 68
Timson, B. S. 58	Waterbury, Saml. 58
Toms, A. P. 45, 154	Waterbury, A. C. 85, 150, 154
Toms, Geo. W. 97, 154	Waterbury, S. R. 85, 150, 154
Toms, Edgar. 98, 155	Waterbury, J. W. 116, 154
Toms, George. 98, 155	Waterbury, Geo. A. 79, 85
Tonar, Barney. 56	Waugh, Dwight. 107
Townsend, O. 45, 58	Weed, Charles. 85
Toepfer, J. A. 56	Weed, Charles L. 85
Totten, W. H. 84, 148	Weed, Alexander. 26, 82
Totten, Hiram. 98	Weed, Alexander H. 107
Todd, G. W. 84	Weed, George W. 73, 99
Todd, C. J. 115	Weed, Levi St. John. 73
Trechardt, John. 58	Weed, John E. 99
Treadwell, C. E. 93	Weed, George. 43, 45, 72
Trowbridge, Wm. H. 7, 92	Weed, Chas. H. 57
Tucker, Henry. 65	Weed, James. 116
Tucker, S. L. 65	Weed, John P. 91
	Webb, J. E. 45
Vail, James. 35, 79, 82, 144	Webb, W. O. 35, 82, 154
Vanderhoff, Jacob. 44, 72	Webb, Allen. 89, 95, 155
Vandervalt, Geo. 101, 149, 154	Webb, Jas. W. 93, 150, 155
Vandervalt, E. 72, 154	Welch, T. M. 89
Vandervalt, John. 47, 53, 154	Welch, James. 116
Vandivere, George. 92	Welch, J. W. 95
Vernal, J. H. 44, 89	Wessels, A. L. 85
Vernal, O. W. 56	White, W. F. 99, 154
Vincent, J. W. 72, 149	Weston, Charles. 98
Vinton, D. H. 105	Whiting, Wm. D. 116
Void, Joseph. 72	Whitney, Geo. E. 116
	Whitney, W. R. 82
Walters, James Henry. ..81, 149, 154	Whitney, H. M. 85
Walters, Charles Conklin. 56, 154	Whaley, Edward. 72
Walters, Edward H. 56, 154	Whaley, John. 65
Walters, John Wesley. 72, 154	Willcox, Wm. C. 107
Walter, Andrew. 115	Wilmot, H. L. 80, 85, 155
Waters, Jacob. 82	Wilmot, Joseph. 88, 155
Waters, John. 35, 88, 150	Wilmot, J. T. 88
Walton, Wm. H. 35, 88, 149	Wilmot, G. W. 88, 154
Walton, Josiah. 93	Wilson, R. 93
Walsh, M. M. 96	Wilson, Robert. 43, 45, 48, 54
Waring, Wm. H. 88	Wilson, John H. 72
Ward, J. D. 57	Wilson, W. J. 98
Wardwell, Chas. W. 7, 33, 107	Wicks, Hercules. 116

Williams, Randolph	93	Yates, James W.	93
Williams, Wm.	72	Youngs, Edward	116, 155
Williams, E. M.	85	Youngs, George W.	54, 155
Wood, S. A.	88	Youngs, J. R.	57, 155
Woolsey, M. B.	116	Youngs, George A.	98, 152
Wright, James	57, 106		
Weed, Edgar S.	108		

CORRECTIONS AND ADDITIONS.

Page 24, line 14, for H. K., read *D. K.*
" 30, " 26, for the States, read *these* States.
" 56, " 13, for Andrew, read *Andrus.*
" 57, " 7. for John A., read John *R.*
" 85, " 27. for Eben R., read Eben *P.*
" 88, all the names between Wm. H. Waring and Geo. H. Meeker, belong to Co. C, 28th Conn.
" 100, " 10. John H. Searles was in the 17th Conn., instead of a N. Y. Regiment
" 113, " 21. for Taylor, read *Gaylor.*
" 114, " 28. for Henry, read *William*

" 55. Charles Bing, from Greenwich, disch. for disability, Feb. 9, 1863.
" 57. Hanford Avery, Co. B, 6th Conn., Feb. 25, 1864.
" 72. Andrew Scofield, Co. B, 17th Conn., July 30, 1862.
" 92. Joseph Holmes, Co. B, 29th Conn. See Obituary.

www.ingramcontent.com/pod-product-compliance
Lightning Source LLC
Chambersburg PA
CBHW030246170426
43202CB00009B/649